Mano-a-Mano

**Fighting the Battle Together
A Devotional for Men and their Teenaged Sons**

By

Bryan, Hunter and Harrison Hall

Copyright © 2009 by Bryan, Hunter and Harrison Hall

Mano-a-Mano
Fighting the Battle Together
by Bryan, Hunter and Harrison Hall

Printed in the United States of America

ISBN 978-1-60791-129-6

All rights reserved solely by the author. The author guarantees all contents are original and do not infringe upon the legal rights of any other person or work. No part of this book may be reproduced in any form without the permission of the author. The views expressed in this book are not necessarily those of the publisher.

Unless otherwise indicated, Bible quotations are taken from The Holy Bible, New International Version®. NIV®. Copyright © 1973, 1978, 1984 by International Bible Society. Used by permission of Zondervan.

Edited by Regina Hall

To contact the authors, you may email us at ossbwh@att.net

www.xulonpress.com

Acknowledgements

We want to say thanks to the following:

- Regina Hall, wife, mother, teacher, editor, friend and helpmeet. You are our paddle and our glue. We love you.
- Kelcie Hall, little sister and big friend. Thanks for putting up with all of our bad jokes, bad moods and bad singing in the car. You have taken eye-rolling to a brand new level.
- Mike Glenn,, Roger Severino, Ken Hindman, Jay Strother, Linc Taylor, Aaron Bryant, Danny Wood, Scott Heath and Jay Watson for the teaching and ministry that you have provided to me and the boys over their teenage years.
- Joy Jordan-Lake, Clifton Lambreth, Tim Steed and Ramon Presson who have all recently travelled this journey.

Contents

1. Responsibility – Take It or Lose It 13
2. Prepared for Battle 21
3. Answering the Call - Yes Lord, I Will!! 29
4. Your Body is a Temple, Not as a Toy 37
5. God's Idea of Male Bonding 45
6. Christ as a Manly Man 53
7. Humility – Eating Humble Pie 61
8. Walk Like a Man, Talk Like a Man 71
9. God – Yes, He Really is That Great! 79
10. Are You Man Enough to Forgive? 87
11. You're In This World, Now Deal With It! 95
12. It's a Matter of the Heart 103
13. Discipline – Oh, That 111
14. Encouragement – Gotta Have Some 119
15. Relationships of a Godly Youth 127
16. Good Deeds for the Do-Gooder 135
17. Hard Work – Sweating It Out 143
18. Greed and Money – It's Not Just the Fat Cats 151
19. When I Run, I Feel God's Pleasure 159
20. Salvation – And the Truth Shall Set You Free 167
21. Salvation – Taking the Road Ahead 175
22. Taking a Stand – Steven's Example 183
23. Taking a Stand – Elijah's Example 191
24. Taking a Stand – Unlikely Heroes 199
25. I Know It's Tempting but……... 207
26. Faith – Go Sit in That Chair 215

27. What Do You Want To Be When You Grow Up - I 223
28. What Do You Want To Be When You Grow Up – II ..231
29. Hang in There – I 239
30. Hang in There - II 247
31. There's No Better Way – Obedience I 255
32. To be Happy in Jesus – Obedience II 263
33. But to Trust and Obey – Obedience III......................271
34. What are You Lookin' at – The Sex talk 279
35. R.E.S.P.E.C.T. — Respecting Others 287
36. We're All in This Together - Fellowship...................295
37. Trust Me? No, Trust Him 303
38. Making Those Tough Choices 311
39. The Unexplained 319
40. Submission to God 327
41. B-Attitudes – Positive 335
42. B-Attitudes - Negative...343
43. Self Confidence – Confidence in the Lord.................351
44. God's Mighty Athletes 359
45. Is This for Real? 367
46. Death Comes Knocking 375
47. Hope for Something Better....................................383
48. Being Prepared – Because You Never Know 391
49. God's Will for us NOW..401
50. Getting in the Word- The Importance of the Bible....409
51. Reaching Out — Helping the Poor..........................417
52. Time to Come Clean - Renewal 425

Introduction

The idea for this devotional came in a very simple setting. I was listening to one of our church ministers describe his vision for discipleship. He hoped that parents would become more personally active and responsible to teach and disciple their children and view the church as a partner in the process rather than a substitute. He went on to say that he had been searching for materials to support families in this process but that he had not found what he was looking for.

I started to examine what I might be able to do to support him. My greatest assets are my family, a wife who supports me and two boys and a girl who challenge me daily. At various times we have used materials for family daily devotionals. There are several very good resources available but our frustration came in the breadth of our needs. There is a six-year difference between our oldest son and our daughter. What is relevant to the oldest may hold little interest for the youngest and vice versa. What works with the guys may be totally inappropriate for my little precious.

In the recesses of my male, militaristic mind came the old battlefield strategy – divide and conquer. Why not focus specifically on where the kids are now. The boys are teenagers and, while they are three years apart, they are going through similar challenges in life. The idea formed: create a devotional for men and their teenage sons that encourages them to focus on issues relevant to their stage in life, as men, and to share God's word together on a consistent basis. I also had a desire to involve the boys in the process so I asked them to join in the project.

What has come out of the process is a weekday devotional. It is divided into weekly or two- week subjects. Given 52 weeks in the year – five days a week — we were looking at 260 daily devotions. We split up the process, each of us taking so an equal share days. I asked the boys to each choose 87 verses or passages that they would like to discuss with me. I then chose 86 that I would like to share with them. I was amazed when very few of the verses overlapped. This gave us a wide range of subjects to discuss. We then split them up into topics of five or ten verses passages.

The boys were asked to comment on the verses they individually chose and then to team up to comment on the verses that I had chosen. The only instruction that I gave them was to pray over each passage and then comment from their hearts and include questions as they had them. During the process I did not dictate or edit their comments, as I wanted them to feel that what they have to say is totally from their heart. My English teacher spouse did edit the grammar, for me as much as for the boys.

I then set to work giving my thoughts on each weekly subject and commenting on the verses and asking questions that I thought might spark conversation. What came out of this was a daily layout of a man's perspective and a young man's perspective with the desire to open up opportunities for discussion, reflection, prayer and discipleship.

We tried to keep the commentary short and provide a daily thought-provoking format that can fit the hectic lifestyle of today's men and young men. This is a format that sometime in the future can be emailed to the men and young men on a daily basis because—well—we figured that was one thing most men do on a daily basis, check their email.

So, who are we? I am not a trained theologian, just a layman who has spent a number of years teaching youth Sunday School and a parent who desires to share the Word of God with his children. The boys are just normal, very active teenagers who love the Lord and want to grow in their faith. The views expressed are mine and the boys' and our prayer is not that we provide some profound work to rival the great writers of Christianity but simply to encourage young men to grow in their faith and to share together with their fathers or other mentors. We recognize that not all young men have a father who will share with them in this manner. We hope, however, that Godly men will step forward to fill the gap and maybe use this same material to provide mentorship and discipleship to these young men.

I also acknowledge that now I need to get to work on something for and with my precious daughter Kelcie, or she will not let me live in peace.

Bryan Hall

With:
Hunter and Harrison Hall

Mano-a-Mano is the title I have chosen

From Wikipedia

Mano-a-mano is a Spanish construction meaning "hand to hand." It was used originally in bullfights where just the matador and the bull confront each other. Current Spanish usage describes any kind of competition between two people where they both compete, but somehow cooperate in achieving something.

****

Men love competition and we know we are in competition for our young men's souls. Men and young men alike are competing but I like the idea of cooperating in the achievement of our goals to become the men that God intends us to be: His men, His mighty warriors, His true and brave allies.

Week 1

Responsibility – Take It or Lose It

One of the myths that seem to be perpetuated in modern society is that young men are incapable of handling tough responsibilities. This expectation of weakness can become a self-fulfilling prophesy that can stunt the emotional and spiritual growth of a young man and leave him without the strength of character needed to become an effective husband, father and leader, even an effective witness for Christ. This week we have chosen several passages that discuss the roots and expectations of God's desire for us as men to take responsibility like men.

You may notice in everyday conversation or through observation that young men may forget or ignore who they are, the fact that they are part of a family and a household. Part of taking responsibility is knowing who you are and how you fit in.

- Men are responsible for upholding God's image of us as a man with unique features and roles.

Another key to taking responsibility is being challenged. Every young man wants to feel important and when they feel that great things are expected of them, it is amazing how they rise to the occasion.

- Men are responsible for managing great things, including the earth and the families that we have been given – external gifts.

Each man is given gifts and talents. Young men should be challenged to discover and be responsible for using those talents responsibly.
- Men are responsible for using the gifts and talents that we have been given - internal gifts.

One way to cripple a young man is by lowering expectations and making excuses for his behavior. Remember back in the day when you fouled someone playing basketball and you were expected to man-up and raise your hand to acknowledge you blew it – instead of arguing, whining and blaming someone else?
- Responsibility for our actions.

Nothing sharpens a young man like facing tough challenges and the expectations that can arise from those tests. God is willing to use young men to overcome tough obstacles and, in supporting them through His love and strength, teaching them to take responsibility in all of life's challenges.
- Responsibility in the face of controversy.

Challenge:
Men: Show support by challenging your young man to take responsibility both in everyday life and as a Christian.
Young Men: Commit yourselves to the challenges God gives you and look for areas in your life where you can step up and gladly take responsibility as men.

Responsibility – Take It or Lose It

Monday

Verse: Genesis 1:27

> *So God created man in his own image, in the image of God he created him; male and female he created them.*

Father's Thoughts: Have you ever noticed that image is the root word for imagination? What an imagination God had to create man. He created us in a unique and varied way. He created us with a purpose and he created us different from woman. He gives us unique responsibilities, unique personalities; we are male, and He meant it that way.

Sons' Thoughts: God wanted us to be unique and individually made, but also wanted us to have many of the same attributes as him. Here, he also tells us that he made humans into two distinct genders, and that they are considered vastly separate.

Discussion Questions: So what does it mean to be both made in the image of God, and male? Given that we are uniquely men, what are our responsibilities as men?

Notes: _____
_____
_____
_____

Tuesday

Verse: Genesis 1:28

> *God blessed them and said to them, "Be fruitful and increase in number; fill the earth and subdue it. Rule over the fish of the sea and the birds of the air and over every living creature that moves on the ground."*

Father's Thoughts: This verse goes to the heart of being a man, right? Power — rule over everything, and go have lots of children. But wait, with great power comes great responsibility, with lots of children comes a ton of responsibility.

Sons' Thoughts: God is telling man everywhere that we should be filling the earth with lots and lots of people. Rule over the earth. This is really the first command that God gives us, and kind of sums up the life of humans.

Discussion Questions: Like nuclear power, like electricity, how do we manage and control the power God has placed in our hands without destroying ourselves?

Notes: _____
_____
_____
_____

Wednesday

Verse: 1 Timothy 4:14

> *Do not neglect your gift, which was given you through a prophetic message when the body of elders laid their hands on you.*

Father's Thoughts: What happens to muscles when they are not used? Atrophy. What happens to athletic skills that are not practiced? They get rusty and slow. You have been given certain gifts, certain skills and certain responsibilities. If you do not use them you will find that they become useless.

Sons' Thoughts: The gifts that God bestows upon us are to be sharpened and used to further the kingdom of God. When people possess a certain talent, yet they don't try hard to make themselves better, they are disobeying God.

Discussion Questions: Write down three things in your life that make you unique. Are you using them for God's glory?

Notes: _____
_____
_____
_____

Thursday

Verse: 2 King's 21:9

> *But the people did not listen. Manasseh led them astray, so that they did more evil than the nations the LORD had destroyed before the Israelites.*

Father's Thoughts: Being a leader is a good thing......if you lead in the right direction. You can also lead right off the edge of a cliff. Whether you are the leader or the follower you need to gauge the direction by God's compass. Through prayer and study, learn to discern motives and potential outcomes so that if you are being led away from the Lord's will you can challenge the direction.

Sons' Thoughts: When people listen to a leader, they must listen carefully to determine whether that person is trying to follow the will of God or trying to promote a selfish agenda. Many cult leaders have very appealing messages, and are usually very good at targeting the right audience. Therefore, you need to keep a sharp eye out when an influential person tells you what to do.

Discussion Questions: Are you bold and strong enough to challenge a leader taking you along a path of destruction? How do you think they will react to your challenge?

Notes: _____
_____
_____
_____

Friday

Verse: Exodus 32:7-9

> *Then the LORD said to Moses, "Go down, because your people, whom you brought up out of Egypt, have become corrupt. They have been quick to turn away from what I commanded them and have made themselves an idol cast in the shape of a calf. They have bowed down to it and sacrificed to it and have said, 'These are your gods, O Israel, who brought you up out of Egypt.' I have seen these people," the LORD said to Moses, "and they are a stiff-necked people.*

Father's Thoughts: Confrontation is difficult but there are times where a man must stand up and face issues head on. God's words to Moses were not "uh-oh, look out, be careful, sneak back to camp', they were "GO DOWN". It was a command to do what a man had to do, confront corruption head-on with a people that did not want to listen to God.

Sons' Thoughts: Here, Moses gives us an inclination of what can happen if we turn our eyes from God and start to rely on man-made objects. When times get rough, we can easily decide to try to take things into our own hands, as the Israelites did here. We start to rationalize things when we should instead turn to God and His appointed leaders for guidance and strength.

Discussion Questions: Are you going to be willing to face opposition and go down to those around you that are "stiff-necked"? Are you willing to be a strong man in the face of controversy at school?

Notes: _____
_____
_____

Week 2

Prepared for Battle

Aggressiveness is clearly a trait of manhood. It has so often been the key to survival; the hunting instinct, the protective nature, the competitive nature of men that is natural and good for us. In certain situations such as sports, play, business and especially in military situations we are encouraged to use that aggressiveness, to harness and control it, to use it for our own good. In other situations, such as at school, inside our homes and in our day-to-day interactions, men are required and encouraged to manage it and keep it under control. We are discouraged from fighting except in extreme cases and sometimes society criticized the male aggressive nature. As Christian men we need to understand and acknowledge that we are at war, a spiritual war that must be fought and must be won. Our instincts for aggressiveness and for preparation are needed and will be put to the test.

God shows us that we have strength and power beyond ourselves and that strength and power comes through Christ Jesus.
- Harness the power.

We need to understand the battle, what we are up against and who we are up against.
- Recognize the enemy.

In spiritual warfare we are called to be prepared. We need to be willing volunteers to aggressively go towards the battlefront, not run the other way.
- Stand, be ready and go.

We need to take the right tools to battle, defensive instruments to protect ourselves from attacks that we know will come, attacks on our character, attacks on our soul.
- We must have a strong defense.

One of the greatest fighting tools that we have in spiritual warfare is our mind. The ability to think and the ability to pray are strong weapons. Combine this with the word of God and you have a strong offensive stand.
- We must present a strong offense with confidence.

Challenge:
Men: Be realistic with your young men on the battles and challenges they will face and what it takes to overcome them.
Young Men: Strive to understand the protective tools God has given us and then learn to channel to weapons God has given you to fight temptation and trials with the aggressiveness you need to overcome.

Prepared for Battle

Monday

Verse: Ephesians 6:10-11

> *Finally, be strong in the Lord and in his mighty power. Put on the full armor of God so that you can take your stand against the devil's schemes.*

Father's Thoughts: We are getting ready for battle. In all the armies of time and in this world, young men have been at the front lines. Do you realize that your grandfathers and their fathers, brothers, uncles who fought in the two world wars were most likely teenagers when they went off to fight for freedom? Young men, you are on the battle lines of a far greater and much more vicious war, the war for men's souls.

Sons' Thoughts: Basically, the Bible is telling us that we can be courageous during any circumstances. We should always know that God will be with us and that we should never be afraid.

Discussion Questions: Are you ready to step up, prepare yourself and become a spiritual soldier? Where are the front lines?

Notes: _____
_____
_____
_____

Tuesday

Verse: Ephesians 6:12-13

> *For our struggle is not against flesh and blood, but against the rulers, against the authorities, against the powers of this dark world and against the spiritual forces of evil in the heavenly realms. Therefore put on the full armor of God, so that when the day of evil comes, you may be able to stand your ground, and after you have done everything, to stand.*

Father's Thoughts: You have to be prepared for a battle. No general in his right mind will send young men to fight unprepared. You need to know who the enemy is and you need to know what his weapons are.

Sons' Thoughts: There are things out there that are trying to break us down, and it is not possible to take them on our own. We cannot be expected to take on evil spiritual forces and succeed. We must rely on the forces of God to carry us through and help us hold our grounds.

Discussion Questions: Who is this spiritual enemy and why is he so dangerous? What does with enemy use as weapons?

Notes: _____
_____
_____
_____

Wednesday

Verse: Ephesians 6:14-15

> *Stand firm then, with the belt of truth buckled around your waist, with the breastplate of righteousness in place, and with your feet fitted with the readiness that comes from the gospel of peace.*

Father's Thoughts: All three of these are important: truth gives you flexibility and freedom of movement, righteousness protects your vital organ, your heart, but let's look at shoes for a minute. Shoes give you a firm foundation; they need to be solid but not heavy. Peace that comes from the good news, the gospel, gives you a firm foundation so that you can keep moving forward.

Sons' Thoughts: We cannot run when Satan attacks us, but stand our ground and face temptation head on. We must not waver in any circumstances but rely on what we know from the Word to use as a defense.

Discussion Questions: Are you confident in your salvation, in the peace that God gives you through Jesus? Is this a firm foundation in your life?

Notes: _____
_____
_____
_____

Thursday

Verse: Ephesians 6:16

> *In addition to all this, take up the shield of faith, with which you can extinguish all the flaming arrows of the evil one.*

Father's Thoughts: The best offense is a great defense. When we are facing fierce battles in our lives, it is our faith that can ward away all of the trials thrown our way. If you let your shield drop, if you lose faith, you are left unprotected; you have lost your defense.

Sons' Thoughts: We need to be willing to stand unwavering when the forces of Satan are propelling temptation into our sight. We must have uncompromising faith and use that as a shield to block what comes our way.

Discussion Questions: Who is attacking you at school? What temptations are coming your way daily? How can a strong faith in Christ help you to deflect these attacks, these temptations?

Notes: _____
_____
_____

Friday

Verse: Ephesians 6:17-18

> *Take the helmet of salvation and the sword of the Spirit, which is the word of God. And pray in the Spirit on all occasions with all kinds of prayers and requests. With this in mind, be alert and always keep on praying for all the saints.*

Father's Thoughts: Satan would love to get into your head. He wants you to doubt, to be frustrated, to give up and give in. Salvation is the protection of our head, our thoughts and our minds. With confidence in our salvation we can resist confusion and doubt and then with the word of God we can fight back and we can conquer.

Sons' Thoughts: A metaphor is being used here to compare the Word of God, prayer and the Holy Spirit to armor which is used to protect someone while they are engaged in battle. We need to remember those who are actually physically in battle to prepare ourselves for the battle that goes on in our own lives.

Discussion Questions: Are you confident in your salvation, are your ready to take God at his word and do battle for what is good, what is true and what is right?

Notes: _____
_____
_____
_____

Week 3

Answering the Call – Yes, Lord, I Will!!

—⚎—

You have all heard the anti-drug slogan, 'Just say NO.' Well, here is the opposite. God has a purpose for each of you. Your life and your actions are very important to God and are at the root of His relationship with you. As young men grow and mature in their faith, they will begin to see how the talents, gifts and desires they are fitted with can be used for God's work. Then all of the sudden, an opportunity presents itself, a chance to do something for the cause of Christ. It may be small, it may be challenging, but it is there and it is all yours. It is at that time you have a choice — will I do it, will I step up to the challenge, and will I take a risk?

The call of God is not reserved for the mature and holy; it can come to the innocent and young.
- Just say "YES"

When we are called by God, to be used by him we are called to action. Very rarely will God call us to monkhood or isolation; we should be bold and active.
- We are called to be witnesses and workers.

Maybe you are called to be a great evangelist or preacher speaking to thousands a night; more likely you will be called to those around you, and those you see every day.
- We are called to be witnesses and workers to individuals.

When we have an opportunity to do a great work for the Lord, we may not be allowed to bask in our glory but be ready to move at a moment's notice.
- We should be prepared to answer the call to move on.

Answering God's call might mean we have to get our of our comfort zone, try something new, take a risk.
- Answering the call may mean a change in direction.

Challenge:
Men: Encourage your young men to examine their lives, to understand that God has a plan for them and that when they are called, they can do fantastic things through Christ.
Young Men: Be ready and be open to God's call. Be prepared to do things for Christ far beyond your expectations and perceived limitations.

Answering the Call - Yes Lord, I Will!!

Monday

Verse: 1 Samuel 3:10

The LORD came and stood there, calling as at the other times, "Samuel! Samuel!" Then Samuel said, "Speak, for your servant is listening."

Father's Thoughts: There are no time limits, no age limits on God's purpose in our lives. God had great plans for Samuel and revealed them to him at a young age. Samuel answered God's call. God's call may come at any time in life; he has called many retirees to start new commitments for Him as well.

Sons' Thoughts: God knows what kind of kid Samuel is, and calls on him to follow and prophecy in his name. Samuel, once he realizes that it is actually God calling him, immediately calls out asking for his instructions.

Discussion Questions: Do you think you are too young to do God's work? Do you think people will doubt you if you tell them you are called by God for specific purposes and actions?

Notes: _____
_____
_____
_____

Tuesday

Verse: Matthew 9:37

Then he said to his disciples, "The harvest is plentiful but the workers are few.

Father's Thoughts: We are now in the third or fourth generation removed from a high percentage of us guys having been raised on a farm. Maybe you remember a grandfather or great- grandfather that still lived the rural life. Before modern machinery, all hands, all family members and whoever else you could get to help would get into the fields and work long, hard hours to bring in the harvest of whatever crops were ready. If there were not enough workers, the crop would remain unharvested and would die and rot. In harvesting the souls of men, we do not want to let any remain to die and rot but instead we want to bring them in to God's great plan. All hands are needed to bring them in.

Sons' Thoughts: This quote of Jesus's really tells us what he expects of us. There are so many people out there who do not understand that the love of God is the empty hole in their life and that it is our duty as believers to share the hope and joy that a relationship with God can bring to someone's life.

Discussion Questions: What kind of hard work do you believe is necessary to witness and to win men's souls for Christ? Why do so many people, even those in the church, seem to fail to show up to work?

Notes: _____
_____
_____
_____

Wednesday

Verse: Acts 8:26-27

> *Now an angel of the Lord said to Philip, "Go south to the road—the desert road—that goes down from Jerusalem to Gaza." So he started out, and on his way he met an Ethiopian eunuch, an important official in charge of all the treasury of Candace, queen of the Ethiopians. This man had gone to Jerusalem to worship,.*

Father's Thoughts: How did God get Philip to do his request so quickly? There was no backtalk, no bargaining, no "okay, whatever!" Son, if you think I am talking about you, I'm not. I struggle just like you do at not being as obedient as I should be, not jumping up, getting on my way and answering God's call to action. But when I do, lives can be changed.

Sons' Thoughts: This passage is telling us how God will put us in the right situations to witness to people. If we obey him, he will set us up for success.

Discussion Questions: Have you heard God's call? Are you ready to answer with your legs?

Notes: _____
_____
_____
_____

Thursday

Verse: Act 8:39

> *When they came up out of the water, the Spirit of the Lord suddenly took Philip away, and the eunuch did not see him again, but went on his way rejoicing.*

Father's Thoughts: When something spiritually great has just happened, it may be tempting to try and sustain the moment, revel in the limelight. Part of answering God's call is moving on to the next task that He has laid out for us. It may require starting over again at the bottom.

Sons' Thoughts: I know personally I am guilty of getting on a spiritual high at church camps and mission trips. It is easy to worship God when we are surrounding by fellow believers focused on the Lord all day. But the test is after these moments, when we are forced to go and face the real world again. Will we fall back to old habits, or keep pressing on towards our Heavenly goals?

Discussion Questions: Have you had a strong spiritual moment at church or at a retreat? Now that it is over are you willing to go back down and start climbing the mountain all over again?

Notes: _____
_____
_____
_____

Friday

Verse: Luke 5:10-11

Then Jesus said to Simon, "Don't be afraid; from now on you will catch men." So they pulled their boats up on shore, left everything and followed him

Father's Thoughts: Our lives have a purpose. Simon thought it was fishing, being a good son and brother. But God called him to be more than that. Was he scared? He must have been terrified because Jesus knows our hearts and He got right to the point with Simon.

Sons' Thoughts: Simon was by occupation a fisherman, but when he hears the Lord calling him to come be his disciple, he realizes that life can only be centered around one thing, and that Jesus's call outdid any other calling that he thought might be relevant in his life, including his source of income. He knows that Jesus will provide for him, and he shows a huge amount of trust as he gives up his whole life to follow Christ. This is what God asks of us daily. He wants us to listen to Him and to have uncompromised feelings towards what He asks us to do.

Discussion Questions: When you receive the call to your highest purpose, will you be afraid? In spite of that fear will you drop everything and follow Him?

Notes:

Week 4

Your Body is a Temple, Not as a Toy

Were you the kind of kid that broke all of his Christmas toys before New Year's Day? Toys, and our own bodies, can be broken and abused if we are irresponsible with them. Young men in their teens are especially vulnerable to abusing the bodies God gave them. As men of God we are called to control our bodies, we are to understand their value to ourselves, those around us and to God. This is not easy with raging hormones and with temptation everywhere. This is why as men of God we need to understand God's expectations and purpose for our bodies and hold each other accountable for how we use them.

Offering our bodies to be used for God's purpose does not happen accidentally or automatically. It takes specific decision and action.
- Offering = Action

Offering our bodies to God means that we become like Him and follow His examples – get on His team.
- Aligning your actions with him

As a Christian, we are constantly being observed by those around us, by other Christians and non-Christians alike.
- Setting an example for others

Offering our bodies means giving it away to be used as God would see fit.
- Using your body to help others

As we grow closer to God then Satan will come at you with all kinds of temptation. Offering our bodies means that we must activity, strongly resist what surrounds us.
- Actively resisting sin.

Challenge:
Men: Teach your young men the value of their bodies. Discuss your own struggles with temptation and commit to support them in theirs.
Young Men: Place a very high value on your bodies, one that cannot be easily "bought". Plan now how to resist the temptations that you will face as a teenager. Commit your bodies fully to Christ and His purpose in your life.

Your Body is a Temple, Not as a Toy

Monday

Verse: Romans 12:1

> *Therefore, I urge you brothers in view of God's mercy, to offer your bodies as living sacrifices, holy and pleasing to God—this is your spiritual act of worship.*

Father's Thoughts: What were sacrifices and why were they important in Jewish and early Christian theology? Sacrifices were the giving up of something valuable and pure as a physical acknowledgement to God that we accepted that we had done wrong. It was meant to repair the broken relationship with God. So what is a living sacrifice? There is nothing more valuable and pure to God than your very soul. When you give that up to God that is true worship.

Sons' Thoughts: Sacrifice. It's something we hear often, whether it be on the playing field or from our parents when we don't want to do something. But have you ever thought of it as an act of worship? I don't believe many of us have. I believe when we hear the word sacrifice, we think of giving up something. But it is so much more a process of gaining. In this case, it's about sacrificing our lives for something so much better.

Discussion Questions: What are some sacrifices you've had to make lately?
Why do you think giving your body is so pleasing to God?

Notes: _____
_____
_____
_____

Tuesday

Verse: Romans 13:14

> *Rather, clothe yourselves with the Lord Jesus Christ, and do not think about how to gratify the desires of the sinful nature.*

Father's Thoughts: We are asked as Christians to "be like Jesus," or to ask "what would Jesus do." When you are competing for a team, you clothe yourself in the uniform for that team. You are identified with the team and you are expected to act in the best interest of the team. Going off on your own and doing whatever you want will cause the team to under perform or lose. You have to focus on what is best for the team and give up yourself to win.

Sons' Thoughts: From tight pants to plaid pants, there are many different fashions in the world today. In a way, the way we dress reflects who we are. I think that's why this metaphor is used. If we so-called "clothe" ourselves with Christ we reflect his love through us.

Discussion Questions: Do you think this is what they mean to clothe your self with Jesus? What kind of effect do you think this "clothing" will have on others' opinion of you?

Notes: _____
_____
_____
_____

Wednesday

Verse: Romans 14:21

It is better not to eat meat or drink wine or to do anything else that will cause your brother to fall.

Father's Thoughts: I once referred to Baptists as "Dunkin' Do-not's". It wasn't as strict when I was growing up, but in my parent's day it seemed that you talked more about what you shouldn't do as a Christian than what you should. It would be easy to backlash on this and feel that it is overly restrictive and should be abandoned. However, as Christians, the world is watching us. The people around you will rightly or wrongly judge you by your actions.

Sons' Thoughts: In this passage Paul speaks about something we don't usually consider most of the time. He talks about causing people other than you to sin. He exclaims that starving yourself would be a wiser choice than to do so.

Discussion Questions: Are there things that you do in your life that may not be wrong for you, that a weaker person might see and if he or she did the same, would weaken them or make them vulnerable to sin? How do you think causing others to sin relates to our own sin? Is it the same/worse?

Notes: _____
_____
_____
_____

Thursday

Verse: Romans 15:1

We who are strong ought to bear with the failings of the weak and not to please ourselves.

Father's Thoughts: If we are healthy and strong this is a great gift that God has given us. Should we then be free to show off, to brag, to use our good health and strength all for our own gain?

Sons' Thoughts: This verse is pretty straight-forward. Since we as Christians have Jesus on our side, we are strong. Not so much physically, but mentally and spiritually. We do not need to use that power for our own good, but in turn use it to help those who are struggling and may need someone to talk to or just to comfort them and tell them they are loved.

Discussion Questions: What are some tangible activities that you can do to use your body for God's work? Can you lift something, move something, and build something for someone who cannot do it themselves? How do you think this could affect those people we help?

Notes: _____
_____
_____
_____

Friday

Verse: Romans 6:11-12

In the same way, count yourselves dead to sin but alive to God in Christ Jesus. Therefore do not let sin reign in your mortal body so that you obey its evil desires.

Father's Thought: When a pest gets in your yard and is tearing up your landscaping or grass you work hard to get rid of it. If a parasite gets into your body, you take antibiotics to kill it so that it does not hurt you further. When something like sin invades us it can tear us up; it can make us less productive and harm our relationship with God. We need to treat that sin like an invader and take tough measures to get it out of our system. Dead to sin is a strong and appropriate reaction.

Sons' Thoughts: Many times in the Bible it says to rid ourselves of sin, the main reason being because it separates us from God and disrupts our daily walk with him. But it also affects the way others perceive us. Sin can cause us to leave a bad impression on people and may hinder us from reaching out to them.

Discussion Questions: What are some of the things that cause you to sin frequently? What does your reaction need to be towards that sin?

Notes: _____
_____
_____
_____

Week 5

God's Idea of Male Bonding

What does it mean to be a friend? Having deep and meaningful friendships with your Christian brothers is an important part of manhood. A friend can be there to lift you up when you are down, can celebrate the greatest moments of your life and can share your deepest thoughts and emotions. The closest of friendships can last as long as you live and can even have a profound impact on generations to come. God gives us both a path to and examples of real friendship between men.

Deep and lasting friendships should be based upon the foundation of God's love.
- God's love is the key to true friendship.

Deep and lasting friendships are not casual part- time habits, they require that we give of ourselves completely.
- True friendship requires the willingness to sacrifice.

Deep and lasting friendships are never one -way streets; they are never selfish or taking.
- A true friend will listen.

Deep and lasting friendships must be built over time with commitment and sacrifice.
- Building strong and lasting friendships.

Deep and lasting friendships can last beyond the initial friends and impact families and even nations.
- True friendships last for generations.

Challenge:
Men: Share with your young men how true friendships have had an impact on your life. Commit to grown in your own friendships as an example.
Young Men: Begin to cultivate friendships that you want to last a lifetime. Take God's examples from His Word as a pattern for great friendships.

God's Idea of Male Bonding

Monday

Verse: 1 John 3:14

> *We know that we have passed from death to life, because we love our brothers. Anyone who does not love remains in death.*

Father's Thoughts: These are pretty powerful words. When we give ourselves to Christ, we are filled with His spirit and are called to love in all circumstances. We may not always like the actions of another person, or they may have hurt us, but we need to give ourselves over to Christ's love through us.

Sons' Thoughts: Death? Did someone just say death? It's not one of those words we usually like to hear. It is most of the time followed by some kind of pain. John must have thought love was a pretty powerful thing to be comparing **not** loving to death. We all want to feel loved.

Discussion Questions: Do we really love our brothers in Christ? Are we willing to show that love through our actions? In your own words, what do you think the true meaning of love is?

Notes: _____
_____
_____
_____

Tuesday

Verse: 1 John 3:16

> *This is how we know what love is: Jesus laid down his life for us. And we ought to lay down or lives for our brothers.*

Father's Thoughts: We should all have great respect of those who serve in our military, our police, our firefighters. They have made a choice that when the time comes they will put themselves at risk to save lives other than their own. They serve with honor. Jesus showed us the ultimate honor. He laid down His life, not just for our bodily safety, but for the safety of our souls. When we get a passion for the souls of men and realize that they are in harm's way, the harm of losing their very souls, then we too should rush into the fire and give of our lives to save the souls of men.

Sons' Thoughts: Brotherly love. It's something we've heard multiple times before. Whether it be a sarcastic remark made by our mothers when we fight with our siblings or even describing the city of Philadelphia. Jesus showed the ultimate sign of love when he died for us. But do you believe you would be able to do the same? I don't know many who would. But laying down our lives for our friends doesn't always have to mean dying for them.

Discussion Questions: Are you passionate enough about men to take the risk? Are you ready to witness for him in spite of the danger? Will you serve with honor? In what other ways do you think we could "lay down our lives" for our brothers?

Notes: _____
_____
_____
_____

Wednesday

Verse: Galatians 6:2

> *Carry each other's burdens, and in this way you will fulfill the law of Christ.*

Father's Thoughts: What does it mean to carry another's burden? Could it be as simple as just taking the time to listen? To have good friends, you need to be a good friend and be willing to inconvenience yourself in order to go out of your way to help a friend.

Sons' Thoughts: We need to work together. As in a tough race, one person out in front all alone cannot hope to run very fast, but when two or more are working together, it can make all the difference in the world, and lead to great things.

Discussion Questions: Who is that best friend? How can you strengthen that and other friendships? How can you carry their load?

Notes: _____

_____
_____
_____

Thursday

Verse: 1 Samuel 20:16-17

> *So Jonathan made a covenant with the house of David, saying, "May the LORD call David's enemies to account." And Jonathan had David reaffirm his oath out of love for him, because he loved him as he loved himself.*

Father's Thoughts: Do you have a best friend? How did you become friends and what are the things that have brought you closer together. Often the best of friends are those who have been through some really tough times with you. You may share difficult moments and your friend has been there to listen, give advice, maybe even tough advice. David and Jonathan went through those tough times together and it made their friendship stronger.

Sons' Thoughts: An intense friendship is something that should be held as a very high priority in your life. Nothing should be able to tear two good friends apart. Jonathan's dad tried to have David killed, but David never blamed Jonathan for anything and their friendship remained strong even through tough times.

Discussion Questions: What do you think it means to love friend as you love yourself?

Notes: _____
_____
_____
_____

Friday

Verse: 2 Samuel 9:6-7

> *When Mephibosheth son of Jonathan, the son of Saul, came to David, he bowed down to pay him honor. David said, "Mephibosheth!" "Your servant," he replied. "Don't be afraid," David said to him, "for I will surely show you kindness for the sake of your father Jonathan. I will restore to you all the land that belonged to your grandfather Saul, and you will always eat at my table."*

Father's Thoughts: Friends for life. David gave us a fantastic example of men's friendships that last a lifetime, and beyond. David loved Jonathan with such deep friendship that it carried on to Jonathan's family. David could have easily ignored the needs of Jonathan's family and "moved on" but instead sacrificed for them and extended his love to them as well.

Sons' Thoughts: Jonathan's sons knows what his grandfather did to David and think that David is going to hold it against him, but instead, his friendship with Jonathan carries down a generation and he regards Mephibosheth as family.

Discussion Questions: Have you begun lifelong friendships? Are your friendships grounded in a deep brotherly love that only God can provide? Are they deep enough to last for generations?

Notes: _____
_____
_____
_____

Week 6

Christ as a Manly Man

—⚹—

We worship a great and awesome God. He is the ruler of all nations, the creator of all living things. With all that greatness, why then would he care about us? Why would he have created humanity and then given us the ability to turn our backs on him, rebel against him? Answers have been sought by many; even King David pondered why God would be "mindful" of us. Yet, not only does he care about us, he loved us so much that God the Father sent his Son Jesus to earth in the form of a man to complete His relationship with us. In this way, we can gain so much confidence in approaching God because Christ became one of us. He had all of the emotions, all of the fears, all of the temptations and all pain that we have as men. He was a MAN.

Jesus did not appear out of thin air as a full grown man. He was born as we all were and grew up dealing with all of the issues young men have to deal with day to day..
- Christ went through the same steps you are going through.

Jesus did not sit on the outside and observe life; he lived it and went through all of life's experiences as a man. Because of this he really knows what living is all about.
- Christ has empathy with us

When we are tempted and we are struggling, isn't fantastic to know we have Jesus who also was tempted. We have His example and we have His strength to overcome available to us.
- Christ endured temptation.

Jesus endured the most painful of situations; there is nothing as a man he held back.
- Christ endured pain.

Jesus not only endured great pain, he suffered the ultimate end of man, He died. And then leading the way, he conquered death.
- Christ endured death.

Challenge:
Men: Lead your young men to an understanding of Jesus as a true and real man, one who knows what being a man is all about.
Young Men: Come away this week with confidence that Jesus understands every aspect of your life so that you can trust Him in all situations that you will ever face.

Christ as a Manly Man

Monday

Verse: Luke 2:52

> *And Jesus grew in wisdom and stature, and in favor with God and men.*

Father's Thoughts: Sometimes it might be easy to forget that Jesus had to go through the same growing stages and pains that we all do. He had to grow up. While this is a short and simple verse it shows us what was important to Jesus in his maturing towards manhood, a dual positive relationship with both God and men. If he had neglected either he would have been incomplete in his maturity and his growth.

Sons' Thoughts: Jesus grew up the same way that we did, and as he began to mature, people realized what kind of person he was. He proved to people that he was a trustworthy person, and men and God learned to love and honor him.

Discussion Questions: What do you feel you need to do to further grow "in favor with God?" What are you doing day to day to build strong relationships with people, both your own age and with those older and younger?

Notes: _____
_____
_____
_____

Tuesday

Verse: Hebrews 2:18

> *Because [Christ] himself suffered when he was tempted, he is able to help those who are being tempted.*

Father's Thoughts: If you are going through a problem, would you rather talk with someone who kind of knows what you might be dealing with, or someone who has faced the same issue and conquered it? For me it is the latter. It is nice to have someone's sympathy but better to have someone's wisdom that came with the scars. Jesus has been there; he bore all our sins and was tempted just like we are.

Sons' Thoughts: Jesus understands us. He went through the exact same temptations as we do. That is why reading what he says in the Bible helps. He gives us advice that we can understand and put to work. And he knows we are not perfect. He only asks that when you do mess up, you come to Him in prayer and ask his forgiveness.

Discussion Questions: Have you come to grips with the manhood of Christ and what that means to you?

Notes: _____
_____
_____
_____

Wednesday

Verse: Hebrews 4:15-16

> *For we do not have a high priest who is unable to sympathize with our weaknesses, but we have one who has been tempted in every way, just as we are—yet was without sin. Let us then approach the throne of grace with confidence, so that we may receive mercy and find grace to help us in our time of need.*

Father's Thoughts: Sometimes I might say to you, "Of course, I understand. I was a teenager myself a loooooong time ago." Being able to sympathize is a powerful bond. It is important to know what someone is going through in order to offer advice or guidance. God is not some far- off distant God because he sent His son in form of a man, a tempted, hurtable, killable man who knows what it is like to be here on earth.

Sons' Thoughts: Jesus understands exactly what we are going through, as he went through the same things himself. As men, we should be able to have the confidence to talk to one another because all of us are, or have, experienced everything at one point in our lives.

Discussion Questions: Why do you think this was part of God's plan to develop a relationship with man?

Notes: _____
_____
_____
_____

Thursday

Verse: Hebrews 12:2-3

Let us fix our eyes on Jesus, the author and perfecter of our faith, who for the joy set before him endured the cross, scorning its shame, and sat down at the right hand of the throne of God.

Father's Thoughts: I remember when I tore my rotator cuff playing racquetball. It was the most intense pain I have ever felt. Then after surgery, the pain was constant and sustained for about another six months. Pain is part of being human and we each have our levels of 'pain tolerance'. Jesus realized he would know pain, pain to the point of death on a cross. Nails in his hands and feet, spear in his side kind of intense pain. Yet contrast that with the constant and sustained joy he had because he knew that the temporary pain he suffered would bring life to us and glory to the Father.

Sons' Thoughts: When we get down, there are many things that people turn to. Some people turn to alcohol, some turn to drugs, but as Christians, we have something that all of us can turn to, and our pain will be heard by Christ, who loves us dearly and wants us to get through whatever it is that is hurting us.

Discussion Questions: Did Christ suffer human pain for you?

Notes: _____
_____
_____
_____

Friday

Verse: Hebrews 2:14-15

> *Since the children have flesh and blood, he too shared in their humanity so that by his death he might destroy him who holds the power of death—that is, the devil—and free those who all their lives were held in slavery by their fear of death.*

Father's Thoughts: Only by experiencing humanity could Christ experience the harshest reality of being human - death. Death is hard to think about when you are young, healthy and looking only at endless dreams and possibilities. It took His death, death on the cross, a despicable, brutal way to die, to give us the key to eternal life. We do not have to fear death anymore. For us older folks, that is more realistic, for you it may be many, many years away but it is still real.

Sons' Thoughts: Let's say there's someone you want to get to know better. What do you do? Well, most of the time in order to understand and relate to that person, you have to put yourself in their shoes and see what they experience on a day to day basis. I believe this is what Jesus did here. He became like his people so that his death would be more real to them. And this plan proved to work as he freed all the lives of the people he had joined.

Discussion Questions: Why do you think Christ had to die for God's plan to be complete?

Notes: _____
_____
_____
_____

Week 7

Humility – Eating Humble Pie

In our adult Sunday School, our teacher suggests that each of the men in the class pray a simple prayer, "Lord, show me myself." That is a really hard prayer to ask because most of us men on the outside try hard to be more than we really are, better than we really are, and then we compare that inflated view of ourselves with others and…..well, you get the picture. Humility is not some fake self -depreciating wimpy outward show. Humility is simply seeing ourselves as God sees us and accepting that we will never be God.

Humility should be the mirror at which we look at ourselves versus a microscope that we take out to examine others.

We should be willing to examine ourselves and be realistic about what we see. Our faith should be how we measure ourselves.
- Lord, show me myself.

When we look at ourselves we need to let God be our judge, not letting the world define what is good or bad.
- Judging by God's standards, not man's.

When we turn our gaze towards others we should refrain from judging their hearts, only God knows for sure.
- Don't point your finger.

When we think of the innocence of a small child, that is how God wants us to approach Him.
- Who is the greatest among you?

Be willing to examine yourself, your motivations, and your heart. Examine others through God's eyes.
- What is your motive?

Challenge:
Men: Guide your young men in knowing the true meaning of humility. Encourage them to examine themselves, but also, lead by your example.

Young Men: Pray the prayer, "Lord, show me myself," and be willing to see yourself through God's eyes. Examine your relationships with others this week and determine if you are following God's ideals for judging others and yourself.

Humility – Eating Humble Pie

Monday

Verse: Romans 12:3

> *For by the grace given me I say to every one of you: Do not think of yourself more highly than you ought, but rather think of yourself with sober judgment, in accordance with the measure of faith God has given you.*

Father's Thoughts: How do we see ourselves? As men, we are usually pretty proud of who we are. We work hard at doing our best, trying to show off and trying to stand out. It can be pretty humiliating when we are brought down to earth by events that show us where we really stand; we lose the game, lose the race, get the bad grade, or lose the fight. God wants us to have a realistic view of ourselves. Not to take it to the extreme and always be negative about ourselves, but to simply see ourselves through His eyes, measuring ourselves by His standard, by our faith in Him.

Sons' Thoughts: Judging is something that has become extremely prevalent in today's "religious" society. We see people and automatically try to think of reasons that we are better than them. We do not have a good relationship with the homosexual community in our country because of how often they hear a Christian tell them that they are not good enough to receive God's love. We should look inward and see in ourselves the immorality and know that we are not worthy of God's love, and that is what makes God's grace so much more amazing than we can imagine. No matter how much someone screws up, they are not immune to God's love and forgiveness and that is where our focus should be, on God's love rather than his wrath.

Discussion Questions: How do you see yourself? How do you compare yourself to others? Are you willing to ask God to show you how he views you?

Notes:

Tuesday

Verse: 1 Corinthians 1:26-29

> *Brothers, think of what you were when you were called. Not many of you were wise by human standards; not many were influential; not many were of noble birth. But God chose the foolish things of the world to shame the wise; God chose the weak things of the world to shame the strong. He chose the lowly things of this world and the despised things—and the things that are not—to nullify the things that are, so that no one may boast before him.*

Father's Thoughts: Young men should be able to relate to this verse. You have not yet started your journey into life, so compared to the world you are still learning, you are still developing. You do not own much of your own property or control too much of your existence outside of your family. In the eyes of the world you still have so much to learn. If you understand where you are and what God has given you today, you can begin to allow him to work through you in any circumstance. Don't compare yourself to others and say, "I cannot," but let God use you as you are and say "I can, through Him."

Sons' Thoughts: God uses anyone available, and that includes people that, by human standards, are inferior or not quite up to par. He continually uses people to break down this idea that some people are superior to others. We all receive God's love and no earthly accomplishment can give us more favor in God's eyes.

Discussion Questions: Even though the world thinks of you only as a young person without much wealth or influence, what can you do to change the world around you for Christ?

Notes:

Wednesday

Verse: Matthew 7:1

"Do not judge, or you too will be judged.

Father's Thoughts: Comparison will always get you in trouble. You want to be better than the other guy so you point out his faults, you point out what he has done wrong, and you judge him and his motives. Don't get me wrong, when someone has sinned and it is outward and visible and destructive, we must confront that, but with love, not judging him as if we are God himself, but leading him to God's mercy.

Sons' Thoughts: This idea is very simple. We should look inward to our own sins and not dwell on others'. Jesus forgave even the adulterer as the religious leaders of the time were trying to stone her, reminding them that no one is without sin.

Discussion Questions: Do you believe the phrase, "judge the sin, not the sinner?" What role should you play in dealing with others' sins? How would you want them to deal with yours?

Notes: _____
_____
_____
_____

Thursday

Verse: Matthew 18:2-3

> *He called a little child and had him stand among them. And he said: "I tell you the truth, unless you change and become like little children, you will never enter the kingdom of heaven. Therefore, whoever humbles himself like this child is the greatest in the kingdom of heaven.*

Father's Thoughts: There is nothing as innocent as a newborn, and nothing as compliant as a small child. Small children will trust and love unconditionally; only later do they learn skepticism and hatred. When we come to Christ, we must be willing to trust him completely, innocently and obediently.

Sons' Thoughts: When a child is told something by an adult, or an older sibling, or anyone else that he looks up to, he usually takes it as fact. The child thinks, "this person has much more experience than I do, so he must be right." This is how God wants us to view him. He wants us to see his commandments, and think to ourselves that God must know best, so I need to comply with what he says.

Discussion Questions: I know this is tough for me as an adult, what about you as a teenager?

Notes: _____
_____
_____
_____

Friday

Verse: Philippians 2:3

Do nothing out of selfish ambition or vain conceit, but in humility consider others better than yourselves.

Father's Thoughts: Man, do I struggle with this. I am guilty of looking at the homeless man, competitors, the guy down the street and saying, "wow, I am better than they are." So many times I approach situations thinking about what I can get vs. what I can offer or give. But I am reminded by this verse that God has a different plan in mind. He wants us to respect the gifts he has given others and to approach them with humility.

Sons' Thoughts: This is going to be a tough one for every guy out there. Society has told us all of our lives to get to the top, and to do it in any way possible. If we need to step on a few fingers to get our way, so be it. God, on the other hand, knows that no worldly possession or skill in any way makes us better than anyone else. Nothing that we can do will make God look down on us and say, "that guy down there really does stand out." God sees all of us as equals, and we should treat everyone with that in mind.

Discussion Questions: How can we as men of God be both strong and humble at the same time?

Notes: _____
_____
_____
_____

Week 8

Walk Like a Man, Talk Like a Man

When a man gives himself to the Lord, what does that mean for how he handles his relationships with his family, with his wife and with his children? The bar is raised because God has expectations of us as men and we should have those same expectations of ourselves. Probably the most pressing issue of our time is the fact that men are not stepping up to the plate when it comes to family. We have become absent fathers, overbearing husbands, and irresponsible in the basic day- to -day care, nurture and leadership of our families. This has to stop! We must take on God's expectations and become the man in the family, with love, strength, courage and conviction.

God has a very specific charge for how men should treat their wives.
- It's right in front of you.

God is just as specific on our relationships with our children.
- Train them up right.

We are given responsibility for our families and we must take this seriously.
- Taking care of what you are given.

As husbands and fathers, we can get distracted and wrapped up in meaningless activity that is not productive.
- Don't waste your time.

God gives us himself as an example of how to do right by our families.
- What are you like and what is God like?

Challenge:
Men: Become that example for your young men on how you deal with family relationships. Get them prepared now for what is expected of them.

Young Men: It is never too early to start becoming the man, husband and father that you want to be. Think of ways that you can prepare yourself for your future.

Walk Like a Man, Talk Like a Man

Monday

Verse: Ephesians 5:25

> *Husbands, love your wives, just as Christ loved the church and gave himself up for her.*

Father's Thoughts: Has anything been so hard to live up to? For God to give us Christ as the example for husbands is a tough act to follow. Christ loves the church totally and completely. Christ gave his life for the church, and not in a pretty manner. But there it is, plain and simple. I know we all fall short of perfection, so we have to look at improvement.

Sons' Thoughts: Well, I can't really relate to the first part of this verse, but I can see that God is saying to us that marriage is very similar to our relationship with God. He wants us to unconditionally love each other and Him. Exclusiveness is something that is necessary in a marriage and also in our relationship with God. We can't expect to put other women ahead of our wives on the priority list and still have a loving relationship, and that goes for God as well. We can't expect to uphold our relationship with God as we continually put other pursuits ahead of Him.

Discussion Questions: What can we do to be better husbands and live up to the lofty example of Christ's love for the church? What can you do now, as a young man, to prepare you to be the best husband you can possibly be?

Notes: _____

_____

_____

_____

Tuesday

Verse: Ephesians 6:4

> *Fathers, do not exasperate your children; instead, bring them up in the training and instruction of the Lord.*

Father's Thoughts: I am sure that I have 'exasperated' you at one time or another. Hopefully, any time I have done so was for good reason: positive discipline, keeping you safe, etc. As an earthly father I am called to be a leader, a teacher, and a mentor. Not just in general life lessons but in the Word and works of the Lord Jesus Christ.

Sons' Thoughts: Again, I don't have children, but I do have a younger brother and sister whom I hope that I have showed them a good example of what living a Christ-like life is supposed to be.

Discussion Questions: How can men do our child-raising job better? How can you as young men help us?

Notes: _____
_____
_____
_____

Wednesday

Verse: 1 Timothy 3:4-5

> *He must manage his own family well and see that his children obey him with proper respect. (If anyone does not know how to manage his own family, how can he take care of God's church?)*

Father's Thoughts: Are we only responsible for our own actions? Not if we have been given responsibility, responsibility for a family, for a marriage, for work in the church. I have often heard the phrase, 'past performance is the best indication of future performance.' Basically, we are judged, and rightly so, by how we have handled responsibility in the past. This may seem harsh, but a man of God is responsible for his family. I don't believe this is a call for perfection, but it is a call to manage wisely, even in the face of controversy.

Sons' Thoughts: The gifts that God bestows upon us are to be sharpened and used to further the kingdom of God. When people possess a certain talent, yet they don't try hard to make themselves better, they are disobeying God.

Discussion Questions: How can you start now to prepare yourself for the responsibility of managing yourself first, and then a family?

Notes: _____
_____
_____
_____

Thursday

Verse: Titus 3:9

> *But avoid foolish controversies and genealogies and arguments and quarrels about the law, because these are unprofitable and useless.*

Father's Thoughts: We sure can waste a lot of time arguing. While the modern church does not argue about genealogies, we have set upon ourselves very deep denominational divides. Even within denominations we have had some very visible splits and controversies that have torn apart the work of the church.

Sons' Thoughts: When people listen to a leader, they must listen carefully to determine whether that person is trying to follow the will of God or trying to promote a selfish agenda. Many cult leaders have very appealing messages, and are usually very good at targeting the right audience. Therefore, you need to keep a sharp eye out when an influential person tells you what to do.

Discussion Questions: How can we break a cycle of petty disagreements in the church and move us towards our true purpose — sharing the Good News with all people?

Notes: _____
_____
_____
_____

Friday

Verse: Luke 11:11-12

> *"Which of you fathers, if you son asks for a fish, will give him a snake instead? Of if he asks for an egg, will give him a scorpion? If you then, though you are evil, know how to give good gifts to your children, how much more will you Father in heaven give the Holy Spirit to those who ask him!"*

Father's Thoughts: I wish that I could say that all fathers have a great relationship with their sons. In the media we hear a lot about bad fathers, fathers that abuse, fathers that harm their families. But by and large men have a tremendous capacity to love their sons. We want you to succeed in all things, school, sports, relationships, and as a Christian father, in your relationship with Christ.

Sons' Thoughts: God does not have a cruel side, and he does not want harm to come to us. Anything that goes wrong is a by-product of our sinfulness and the consequences go way back to Adam and Eve.

Discussion Questions: Think about your relationship with your earthly father. What does he do to show you his love?

Notes: _____
_____
_____
_____

Week 9

God – Yes, He Really is That Great!

Last time I looked, no man could create a mountain. Sure, with a little bit of dynamite, even a nuclear device, man can somewhat destructively alter what God has made, but create it, never. It is such a mystery to us that God, who has made us and all that surrounds us, has chosen to have a relationship with us. Just that thought should bring us to our knees. Young men have a tendency to want to go against the norm, to buck authority and to stretch their independence. As you discover yourselves as young men, those things will happen (just stay inside the law, okay), you will want to do things differently than your parents, show you are unique. Understand though, that it is the powerful, almighty God that made you unique in the first place. Learn to respect and revere Him, to trust and obey Him and you will have independence with great power, an independence to become the kind of man He wants you to be – a Godly man of power.

While we may change our minds constantly or waiver and waffle on what we believe, God is not like that. He is always consistent.
- God is unchanging and compassionate.

The God of the Old Testament is the same God we worship. We should give Him the same respect He was given back then.
- God is everlasting and powerful.

Who He is dictates what we should be like, not the other way around.
- God wants us to be like Him— holy.

He made you and me and everything about us is His. We need to understand that and respect His desires.
- God made us, He commands respect.

Because God does not change, He does not need to worry about time, he is forever.
- God is forever.

Challenge:
Men: After looking into your own heart and getting right with God, teach your young men the awe and honor afforded by our Great God.

Young Men: Learn to respect God's power. Learn to respect both the honor that your relationship with the Almighty God brings as well as the responsibility required of you as a man serving such a Great God.

God – Yes, He Really is That Great!

Monday

Verse: Malachi 3:6

> *"I the LORD do not change. So you, O descendants of Jacob, are not destroyed.*

Father's Thoughts: I like change; I like the excitement of a new assignment at work, a new project, a new challenge. But I have to be careful that liking change does not make me unreliable and inconsistent in my relationships. God, however, does not change. He is consistent, loving, powerful and just. Because of this, we can trust him.

Sons' Thoughts: God shows his compassion and his holiness by never changing. He will continue to love us no matter what we do to him.

Discussion Questions: Why do you think God wanted to assure us that He does not change? What are those things in your life that are better because He does not change?

Notes: _____
_____
_____
_____

Tuesday

Verse: Exodus 3:6

Then he said, "I am the God of your father, the God of Abraham, the God of Isaac and the God of Jacob." At this, Moses hid his face, because he was afraid to look at God.

Father's Thoughts: History should be important to us. It is good for us to know that the same God we serve is the God of history and the God of our forefathers. In this way we should respect God, His strength and His consistency, and we should be in awe of His power. Our reverence and fear (respect) of God should be like Moses'.

Sons' Thoughts: The sheer power of the voice of God is enough to scare someone so much that they will hide their face and quiver in fear. This is the power and strength of God in comparison with mortal man.

Discussion Questions: Do you grasp how powerful God really is? Do you respect Him as the God of all ages and of all people? How can you show that respect in your daily life?

Notes: _____
_____
_____
_____

Wednesday

Verse: Leviticus 19:2

> *Speak to the entire assembly of Israel and say to them: 'be holy because I, the Lord your God, am holy'.*

Father's Thoughts: God is God. He is the great I AM. He is unchanging, loving and mighty. He is holy. He asks us to take on that characteristic, to be like Him. That is a tall order. I believe this is why God had Moses speak this to the "entire assembly". Being holy is not something we can approach lightly, or alone. We must surround ourselves with others who are also striving to be holy, encouraging one another. Only through Christ can we make that journey to holiness.

Sons' Thoughts: God puts it very simply here. He says, "if I can do it, you can do it." He obviously knows that we can't live a perfect life, but he at least expects us to try.

Discussion Questions: Discuss what you thing it means to be holy? Are you on a journey towards holiness?

Notes: _____
_____
_____
_____

Thursday

Verse: Exodus 4:11-12

> *The Lord said to him, "Who gave man his mouth? Who makes him deaf or mute? Who gives sight or makes him blind? Is it not I, the Lord? Now go, I will help you speak and will teach you what to say."*

Father's Thoughts: So often I fight God with the first words being "I can't." But God says to us "I can!" If we truly trust Him and give ourselves over to His purposes then he will provide the way to overcome our weaknesses.

Sons' Thoughts: Moses is doing something that a lot of us do a lot of the time. I know that I give excuses as to why I don't need to do my chores, why I don't need to read my Bible, and why I don't need to do exactly what the Bible says. God looks at us and says, "I don't want to hear it. Without me, you wouldn't even be here, and you wouldn't be asked to do these things anyway." This reminds me of another verse that says, "With God, all things are possible."

Discussion Questions: When have you doubted yourself? When was the last time you told God or others 'I can't' or 'I'm not good enough?'

Notes: _____
_____
_____
_____

Friday

Verse: Hebrews 6:16

> *Men swear by someone greater than themselves, and the oath confirms what is said and puts an end to all argument.*

Father's Thoughts: There is that moment in math class that each of you will get the concept of infinity. That endless loop that goes on and on. When studying astronomy, there will be the day you realize the vastness of the universe that God has created. There will be that moment when dissecting a frog, a cat, a pig, that you realize how complex life is and just how awesome must be the One that created it. Then hopefully there will be the moment that you realize just how awesome and great God is and when you give your all over to him — wow — end of argument. God is Great.

Sons' Thoughts: This is why there is no reason for anyone to get to heaven and say, "But I never even heard of you." Anyone can look around and see the vastness of our world and everything in it, and realize that it was not an accident.

Discussion Questions: What do you see around you that points to the greatness of God? How can these things help to give you confidence in God?

Notes: _____
_____
_____
_____

Week 10

Are You Man Enough to Forgive?

Revenge is sweet…..revenge is best served up cold…...many men feel this way and believe that it is a masculine or manly thing to get back at someone who has wronged them or hurt them is some way. God has a very different thought on the subject. Forgiveness is at the root of our Christian faith; God has forgiven us of our sins, and now he asks us to forgive others in the same way. We need to learn from Jesus the basics of forgiveness and apply them in our lives, to make it a deep understanding and to be man enough to overcome our own feelings of right, wrong and justice and take on His thoughts and take on His ability to forgive.

God knows our very thoughts and will challenge our thinking. Would you like to answer a question that Jesus himself asks?
- Jesus asks a question.

Now we get to hear the answer from someone whom Jesus asked a question. Is it the same answer you would have given?
- The answer.

What are the basics of forgiveness?
- What are we supposed to do?

How does unforgiveness affect our relationship with God?
- Clean out the drawers.

Forgiveness is an activity, not a passive thing. It requires that you get both the heart in order and that you work with the one you are forgiving as well. He might just need your help.
- Forgiveness is action.

Challenge:
Men: Lead by example and this should be a very valuable bonding time. Maybe you need to forgive your young man, maybe there is someone in your life you need to forgive.
Young Men: The very nature of your age will test this lesson in your life. As a young man you will have ample opportunity to be "wronged or 'dissed.'" Let God teach you the ability to forgive, let Jesus be your example.

Are You Man Enough to Forgive?

Monday

Verse: Luke 7:40-42

> *Jesus answered him, "Simon, I have something to tell you." "Tell me teacher," he said. Two men owed money to a certain moneylender. One owed him five hundred denariis, and the other fifty. Neither of them had the money to pay him back, so he cancelled the debts of both. Now which of them will love him more?"*

Father's Thoughts: This will be short. Pretend you are Simon, answer the question.

Sons' Thoughts: Jesus is saying that God will cancel our debts and forgive those who have sinned against him, no matter the size of the sins that they committed.

Discussion Questions: Spend some time together discussing your answers. What do you thing that you "owe" to God?

Notes: _____
_____
_____

Tuesday

Verse: Luke 7:43

> *Simon replied, "I suppose the one who had the bigger debt cancelled." "You have judged correctly," Jesus said.*

Father's Thoughts: Salvation is equal for all. Eternal life is a gift that is given to all those that come to God through Christ Jesus. There may be those, however, that look at themselves and say 'Hey, I wasn't that bad." They may be right, maybe if there were "levels" of sin they could be proud that they kept it on the high side. That is a matter of the heart. Then there is the man who absolutely knows he is the world's worst sinner. He cannot look at a mirror without being disgusted with himself.

Sons' Thoughts: The one with the bigger debts would of course be the most grateful, and that is why many people who have lived very immoral lifestyles and then come to know Christ are some of the most devoted Christians out there. They felt like no one could forgive them for what they have done, and when they hear what Christ offers, they love him to their fullest.

Discussion Questions: What does forgiveness mean to this man? Are you that man? Are you rejoicing in your cancelled debt?

Notes: _____
_____
_____
_____

Wednesday

Verse: Colossians 3:13

> *Bear with each other and forgive whatever grievances you may have against one another. Forgive as the Lord forgave you.*

Father's Thoughts: Patience, Patience, God please give me patience, NOW! Maybe I should turn this around, Patience, Patience, God, have patience with me, PLEASE! God has been patient with us. He gave his only son as a fulfillment of that patience. Now it is our time to have patience with our brothers (both literal and figurative, guys) and learn how to forgive in the long term.

Sons' Thoughts: Forgiveness is one of the toughest things we as humans have to deal with. We have the urge to get back or get even with the person who wronged us so that they may feel the pain we dealt with. We need to pray for the Lord's help in sending this urge below and suppressing it there, so we may learn to forgive as Christ ultimately forgave each and every one of us.

Discussion Questions: Have you been patient enough, long enough, to forgive whoever has wronged you? What happened to your friendship after you were able to forgive them?

Notes: _____
_____
_____
_____

Thursday

Verse: Mark 11:25

> *"And when you stand praying, if you hold anything against anyone, forgive him, so that your Father in heaven may forgive you your sins."*

Father's Thoughts: What can block us from what we desire? Is it that 270 lb lineman that pounds us into the turf when we try and make the tackle? Is it that relay handoff that fell to the ground? Is it that teacher that we never really understood?

Sons' Thoughts: Sometimes we might take it for granted that God forgives us constantly for what we do wrong. But that's not all there is to it. If we don't forgive others when they do us wrong, then why do we expect to be forgiven when we screw up? We need to learn to forgive others and I promise, it'll lift a big load off of our shoulders when we do.

Discussion Questions: What stands in the way of that great relationship with God through Christ? Could it be bitterness in our hearts left by unforgiveness? Are you a grudge holder?

Notes: _____
_____
_____
_____

Friday

Verse: Galatians 6:1

> *Brothers, if someone is caught in a sin, you who are spiritual should restore him gently. But watch yourself, or you also may be tempted.*

Father's Thoughts: The Bible never lets us sit around and bask in our own glory. Part of forgiveness is restoration. If you are spiritually strong, you have an obligation to active forgiveness, to get right there with that person and help to pull him out of his sin. But there is a warning. Approach this with prayer and possibly in numbers because to pull someone out of the mud you may have to go in after him.

Sons' Thoughts: We always want to make friends. Part of our nature wants to belong and just hang out with people. But, we must also be careful of the people we choose to chill with. Are they doing stuff that might not have the best influence on us? Are they possibly causing us to question our faith or beliefs? This verse does not warn against helping those people, just cautions us not to fall into temptation while at it.

Discussion Questions: What are some ways that you can join with others who are spiritually strong so that together you can help others?

Notes: _____
_____
_____
_____

Week 11

You're In This World, Now Deal With It!

There is a friend of the boys who is in two hard core/metal style bands. This young man is one of the strongest Christians in the school and has taken that strength and chosen to be right in the middle of non-Christians and to be a witness. This can be hard to do but it is more realistic to what a man will face in life than isolating yourself and pretending the non-Christian world does not exist. As you mature as Christians, you will be able to deal more and more with a world that is hostile to our beliefs. Christ crucified, raised from the dead, and a loving God who cares for us are not messages the world embraces easily. We need to understand the world, learn to live in the world but not let the world control us.

What is the difference between the 'world' and what God has as an ideal for us?
- What does this world have to offer?

We all live with what goes on around us. There are many pressures for us to do things like everyone else does them.
- Should we be like the world?

Well, we are here; God does not take new Christians out of their world and isolate them, so how do we make our way through the day- to- day world.
- How does God want us to deal with the world?

Christians are called to be different and because of this the world may not treat us the same way, they may not like the message we bring.
- How does the world treat us?

We are here to stay until God calls us home or Jesus returns. So we need to know, need to have a plan, how we should live in this world and how God wants us to handle our relationships, especially our deepest ones.
- How should we live in this world with others?

Challenge:
Men: You know what it is like to live in a world that might be hostile to Christians. Teach your young men how to approach the world and relationships that will help them spread the word to the world, but not be corrupted by it.
Young Men: Start now while you are young planning on how you deal with what the world will throw at you. Develop a strategy for life on how you will deal with the world's hostility, temptations, and attractions while keeping yourself from becoming like it.

You're In This World, Now Deal With It!

Monday

Verse: 1 John 2:16

> *For everything in the world—the cravings of sinful man, the lust of his eyes and the boasting of what he has and does—comes not from the Father but from the world.*

Father's Thoughts: Look around us. Television, advertising, pro sports all are full of stumbling blocks. I know that I am guilty of laughing at things I should be ashamed of, enjoying things I should turn away from. The other day I had my sunglasses on and, because they altered my depth perception, I had a hard time walking on uneven ground. The world can alter our perception and cause us to stumble and fall.

Sons' Thoughts: Where we live, the friends we have, and the choices we make all affect our actions. Sometimes when people mess up they say it was their "sinful nature" and try to blame it on forces out of their control. But God says this isn't the case. He truly spies the object that causes us to sin-the world.

Discussion Questions: What real world choices do we make that can cause us to stumble? Have you ever heard someone say their messing up wasn't their own fault? How did you respond?

Notes: _____
_____
_____
_____

Tuesday

Verse: Romans 12:2

> *Do not conform any longer to the pattern of this world, but be transformed by the renewing of your mind. Then you will be able to test and approve what God's will is—his good, pleasing and perfect will.*

Father's Thoughts: One of life's biggest questions is: "How will I know God's will?" It starts with conforming your mind to God's standards (remember—Love, Joy, Peace, Patience....see Galatians 5:22 when you have a free moment). Conforming to the world around us robs us of these fruits and puts us farther from God and farther from His good, pleasing, and perfect will.

Sons' Thoughts: How can we hear God's voice? We don't really hear much today about people seeing visions or having God speak to them, unless you walk down to your local psychiatric ward. In these days, it takes a lot of just clearing your mind and listening in order to know God's plan for you. But first, as the verse says, we must turn from the world and focus on God.

Discussion Questions: Can you shake off the hatred, pessimism, restlessness, etc. that surrounds us? How can we as REAL men help each other to accomplish this?

Notes: _____
_____
_____

Wednesday

Verse: 1 John 5:3-4

> *This is love for God: to obey his commands and not be burdensome, for everyone born of God overcomes the world. This is the victory that has overcome the world, even our faith.*

Father's Thoughts: Dealing with the world and all it has to offer comes down to the same thing, obedience. Being born into God's family through faith in Jesus Christ gives us this victory to deal with the world, to overcome its temptation. Yes, we have to live here and face it day to day, but we have a way through.

Sons' Thoughts: You might have wondered before "God loves me so much, how can I ever return the favor in such a meaningful way?" Well, here's your answer. This verse simply states that the best way to show God you love him is to obey his commands.

Discussion Questions: I know a lot of your friends are struggling too. Have you told them lately how they can be victorious? Have you shown them how?

Notes: _____
_____
_____
_____

Thursday

Verse: 2 Corinthians 7:10

> *Godly sorrow brings repentance that leads to salvation and leaves no regret, but worldly sorrow brings death.*

Father's Thoughts: There is a big difference between truly being sorry and……..being sorry you got caught. When the second one is your primary feeling, you will tend to put all your effort into finding your way around the restriction and not getting caught the next time. What a sad, sad path to choose. Jails are full of second offenders that thought they would just do the crime better the next time. True repentance, deep down, heart felt regret is the process of turning away from the sin you have committed and dedicating yourself to living your life for Christ. It is this true repentance that leads to a relationship with the living God, salvation, and eternal life.

Sons' Thoughts: We've all been to a funeral before. Whether we really knew the person or not, we always feel some sort of sorrow that another life has ended. But if we dwell on death so much, and it clouds our thoughts, it can be dangerous. We start thinking thoughts we don't want to and become frightened, and soon it could become part of us. This is what this verse is warning us about. Mourning over the loss of a loved one is natural, but it should not consume us.

Discussion Questions: What do you think it means to leave "no regrets?" What do you think is meant by Godly sorrow?

Notes: _____
_____
_____
_____

Friday

Verse: 2 Corinthians 6:14

> *Do not be yoked together with unbelievers. For what do righteousness and wickedness have in common? Or what fellowship can light have with darkness?*

Father's Thoughts: Yoking is different from casual acquaintance. When you are yoked with someone, that is as close as it gets. I could refer to the deepest of friendships, business partnerships, even marriage. As Christians, we are called to be out among the world, to be witnesses to the lost, yet we need to be careful in choosing our most intimate relationships so that we do not surround ourselves with additional temptation.

Sons' Thoughts: Yes, I know. It said yoked. And what does that mean? In olden times, cows or oxen pulling something would be held together by what they called a "yoke." So it called for the cows to be uncomfortably cramped together. So what would happen if one of them fell? Well, the other one would go down with it. That's what this verse is saying will happen if we get too close to those who have bad influences on us. We could become more and more like them without realizing it. And by the time we do, it could be too late.

Discussion Questions: Who are those people around you that you give the most of yourself to? Are they a positive or negative influence on you? How could we keep ourselves from falling into an unequally yoked situation?

Notes: _____
_____
_____
_____

Week 12

It's a Matter of the Heart

I have known many fakes in my life. I will try not to judge them but I can observe their actions. I have heard men who will say wonderful things in public, when people are watching, and then they turn ugly and nasty when not in the public eye. People can fake the outside and can do a pretty good job at fooling people for awhile. But God is not fooled; He looks into our deepest thoughts, our desires and our motives and judges us by what is in our hearts, not what we show on the outside for public consumption. God truly wants to change us from the inside out, he wants to deal with our hearts and minds first and then let us reflect the inner beauty of His love on the outside for the world to see.

What you are inside, your thoughts, your fears, your desires, are your true reflection. You may put on a front in public but you are what you think, feel, and love in your heart.
- Heart as a mirror

You can say anything you want, but what you most desire defines you.
- What lies in the heart

What is in your heart will eventually come out in your actions, good or bad.
- A heart divided

When we truly ask Christ into our heart and give it over to Him, he can direct us and shape us into our highest potential
- An undivided heart

Christ is willing to work with us to change our hearts even as hard as they might have been before.
- A new heart

Challenge:
Men: Help your young men to understand that the outward appearance can be faked but what is deep in your heart will be what eventually controls them.

Young Men: Look deep into your heart, look at your motives, your fears and your desires. Begin to give them fully over to Christ and let him change you from the inside out.

It's a Matter of the Heart

Monday

Verse: Proverbs 27:19

As water reflects a face, so a man's heart reflects the man.

Father's Thoughts: Look in the mirror. You see the imperfections, the blemishes, the flaws. You see your own eyes, you can see every expression. There is no denying who you are when you see your own reflection. Who you are deep down inside, in your very heart, is the true reflection of your character. Don't kid yourself into thinking you can fool those that truly look deep into your heart. They will see the true you.

Sons' Thoughts: "When will my reflection show who I am inside?" These words from Mulan (greatest animated movie ever) are spoken by a young girl who is being looked down upon because of her appearance. But I think it relates to every one of us. We are all guilty of judging others from the outside. In that same way, we must also search our own hearts to find out who we really are.

Discussion Questions: What are you reflecting outward from your heart? How do you think others see you?

Notes: _____
_____
_____
_____

Tuesday

Verse: Matthew 6:21

For where your treasure is, there your heart will be also.

Father's Thoughts: My dad had a friend from his home town that was the most sought after Sunday School teacher at the First Baptist Church. When we would visit, my dad noticed that almost all his lessons dealt with money, wealth and possessions, and not in a very healthy way. Eventually through his lust for money, the man lost his business, his family, his reputation, his dignity and his freedom because he let greed dictate his life.

Sons' Thoughts: Let's get straight to the point. We all love our iPods, our TV's, our cars. We love having the biggest and best out of all of our friends. But there's a point when having nice things becomes an obsession. So be aware so you can stop these things from slowly taking hold of your life.

Discussion Questions: Are you letting something you treasure more than God dictate your heart? How should you treat that something?

Notes: _____
_____
_____
_____

Wednesday

Verse: Luke 6:45

> *The good man brings good things out of the good stored up in his heart, and the evil man brings evil things out of the evil stored up in his heart, for out of the overflow of his heart his mouth speaks.*

Father's Thoughts: I know of people who have storm shelters in which they have stocked food to tie them over in case of an emergency. What if the crisis occurred and the family got into the shelter only to find out that all the food that was stored there was rotten? So it is with our hearts. Whatever resides there is what we will have to live off of and is what we will have to share with others.

Sons' Thoughts: The gifts that God bestows upon us are to be sharpened and used to further the kingdom of God. When people possess a certain talent, yet they don't try hard to make themselves better, they are disobeying God.

Discussion Questions: What are we storing up for the day of crisis? Are they good things, or evil? Is it love, or hatred?

Notes: _____
_____
_____
_____

Thursday

Verse: Psalm 86:11

Teach me your way, O LORD, and I will walk in your truth; give me an undivided heart, that I may fear your name.

Father's Thoughts: "Give me an undivided heart". When someone wants your undivided attention they want you to put aside all outside distractions, shut out the rest of the room, the rest of the world. David was a 'man after God's own heart' but he would occasionally let things distract him: politics, family issues, women. We all have these and other things that get in the way.

Sons' Thoughts: There are so many things in our daily lives that can distract us, whether it's grades, sports, or girls. But be sure, in all the hustle and bustle, not to shut God out of your thoughts.

Discussion Questions: What can you do the 'unite' your heart for God so that you can walk in his truth and fear his name?

Notes: _____
_____
_____
_____

Friday

Verse: Ezekiel 36:26-27

> *I will give you a new heart and put a new spirit in you; I will remove from you your heart of stone and give you a heart of flesh. And I will put my Spirit in you and move you to follow my decrees and be careful to keep my laws.*

Father's Thoughts: Do you know the term "attitude check"? That is what God wants us to do, have an attitude check on ourselves. Sometimes as men we can get all knotted up inside and everything that we think about is negative. We get so hardened with bad attitudes that no one can get inside us. Maybe it's a defense mechanism. Regardless, it turns our hearts into stone. God wants us to loosen up to him and let Him inside our hearts. He wants to give us His Spirit who will bring a positive change and encourage us to follow Him.

Sons' Thoughts: If someone has ever thrown a rock at you, you probably noticed pretty quickly that they aren't the softest things in the world. The metaphor of having a heart of stone is used many times throughout the Bible. It is used to show that the person is well-set on their way of thinking and not liable to be persuaded otherwise. God says he will remove this kind of heart and replace it with one that will be more open-minded to His will and not our own.

Discussion Questions: What things in your life are causing you to be defensive, to harden yourself to God and to others?

Notes: _____
_____
_____
_____

Week 13

Discipline – Oh, That

—∞—

Is there anyone who can really say they enjoy being disciplined? Discipline has such a broad connotation since it can range from a loving guiding hand to a harsh punishing hand. We can get so wrapped up in the method of discipline that we can forget the purpose of it. In the human sense, discipline of a parent or other adult to a child is meant to correct when an action is taking you in a bad direction, punish when you have crossed the line into the dangerous or unhealthy, or teach when there is something important for you to know or follow. This is really not much different from God's discipline, yet His is eternal, spiritual, and always for our good. As earthly fathers we will make mistakes in the way we discipline. Sometimes it will be out of anger or frustration and may not provide perfect guidance. My only prayer is that the discipline you receive from me is given in the spirit of my relationship with Christ and that you will respect me for it in the long run. However, God's discipline is ALWAYS out of love, will lead you towards a deeper relationship with Him, and provide you the tools to meet your highest purpose in His kingdom.

Through our relationship with Christ, God's only Son, we are also now brought in to the family as sons with all of the privileges, including discipline.
- Disciplined as sons

God does not see us as some evil stepchild. He loves us as His very own kids.
- Legitimate Children

After the pain is over, a loving father's discipline should earn your respect, God's discipline should earn your awe.
- Respect of discipline

When we receive the Lord's discipline we should strive to understand that it is meant to help us in the long run.
- Painful today, purposeful tomorrow

Self-discipline is the sign that you have learned your lesson well. Start by applying it to one of the toughest aspects of your life, what you say.
- Applied learning

Challenge:
Men: Understand the role of earthly father and mentor when it comes to discipline. Begin to measure your discipline with that of the Father so that your instruction will be pleasing to him and helpful to your young man.

Young Men: As young men, learn how to take discipline in the most positive way. Although it may not seem great at the time, use the lessons to become stronger so you can strive for self-discipline.

Discipline – Oh, That

Monday

Verse: Hebrews 12:5-6

> *And you have forgotten that word of encouragement that addresses you as sons: "My son, do not make light of the Lord's discipline, and do not lose heart when he rebukes you, because the Lord disciplines those he loves, and he punishes everyone he accepts as a son.*

Father's Thoughts: You are part of an earthly family. Every family has rules and every family has codes of conduct that are unique to being part of that family. People that are outside of the family may not be subject to those rules, but they are also not privileged with the good things the family brings, the unique love and relationships. Even better, when you accept Christ as your savior, you become part of the family of God.

Sons' Thoughts: No one likes being punished. But the main reason our parents discipline us is because they love us. They want us to learn a lesson that will help us in the future. This verse is saying that God punishes out of love also, and does it to everyone who believes in Him.

Discussion Questions: Are you ready to accept both the love and the discipline to go along with being part of the family of God?

Notes: _____
_____
_____

Tuesday

Verse: Hebrews 12:7-8

> *Endure hardship as discipline; God is treating you as sons. For what son is not disciplined by his father? If you are not disciplined (and everyone undergoes discipline), then you are illegitimate children and not true sons.*

Father's Thoughts: I love you boys. Why then do I sometimes seem harsh and unyielding? It's because I want to look beyond the moment and teach you things that will make you better men. I'm just an earthly father so God's discipline is infinitely better and more productive than mine. His motives are pure love. He wants you to grow into men that He can be proud of, men that will do His will and change lives for His kingdom.

Sons' Thoughts: We all know someone whose parents never get them in trouble. They never change their attitudes because they don't know any better. They keep on being disrespectful to people because they don't believe there will be any consequence. They end up getting themselves into a whole lot more trouble than they knew was possible. This is why we are disciplined. So we can avoid those circumstances.

Discussion Questions: Are you ready to submit to God's teaching, His perfect discipline, so that you can grow up to do marvelous things for Him?

Notes: _____
_____
_____
_____

Wednesday

Verse: Hebrews 12:9-10

> *Moreover, we have all had human fathers who disciplined us and we respected them for it. How much more should we submit to the Father of our spirits and live! Our fathers disciplined us for a little while as they thought best; but God disciplines us for our good, that we may share in his holiness.*

Father's Thoughts: Well....I hope you respect me for it. My discipline was usually narrow, to keep you safe. God's discipline is much deeper, it is meant to help you share in his holiness.

Sons' Thoughts: You might not be to the point yet where you respect your father for his groundings or spankings. I know, they hurt. But once you realize what they did for your character, you will better embrace the discipline God will keep on giving.

Discussion Questions: What do you think it means to be holy, like He is holy?

Notes: _____
_____
_____
_____

Thursday

Verse: Hebrews 12:11

No discipline seems pleasant at the time, but painful. Later on, however, it produces a harvest of righteousness and peace for those who have been trained by it.

Father's Thoughts: I really do not like to be punished, criticized, disciplined. I have more pride than is good for me so I tend to not take it well. It is comforting to know that through discipline I am being trained and groomed for a better purpose. Although you are currently under adult supervision, with the discipline that comes from that, I hope you will learn to accept lessons learned and grow stronger in your faith and in your walk with God.

Sons' Thoughts: Here it is again. The great message telling us to accept discipline and allow it to make us become a better person.

Discussion Questions: Do you believe that God's discipline if fair and just?

Notes: _____
_____
_____
_____

Friday

Verse: James 3:7-8

> *All kinds of animals, birds, reptiles and creatures of the sea are being tamed and have been tamed by man, but no man can tame the tongue. It is a restless evil, full of deadly poison.*

Father's Thoughts: How many times have you just hauled off and popped somebody in the jaw? You know, just turned around and gave them a good one, maybe broke a couple of their teeth, blackened their eye? I am sure you would look at me with horror and say, "I would never do that." Okay, maybe you have that under control, but then I ask, "How many times have you talked about someone behind their back, yelled at them, swore at them, maybe an offhand remark that crushed their spirit, hurt their feelings? I doubt you can control that to the same degree.

Sons' Thoughts: I remember when I was younger one of my teachers saying "The tongue is the strongest muscle in the body." And I thought to myself, "That can't be true." But I had misunderstood her. What she meant is that whatever comes out of your mouth can hurt people emotionally a whole lot more than you could hurt them physically.

Discussion Questions: How DO you tame the tongue?

Notes: _____
_____
_____
_____

Week 14

Encouragement – Gotta Have Some

—⚏—

Is there any man alive that cannot say he has been down and discouraged at one time or another? I know I have and not in simple ways. Feeling down on yourself can be extremely complex and can be a source of frustration and depression. Maybe I feel so strongly about encouragement because I need it so badly. I love a pat on the back for a job well done, an uplifting word when I am tired and may not want to do something that I know I need to do. Then there are the very serious times, times where I feel I am at the end of my rope and cannot find a way around a problem or issue in my life. That is when the voice of a Christian brother can mean the world to me, reminding me of the hope of Christ and that my Father in heaven loves me. Then there is the other side of the coin. There is a responsibility that I have to be an encourager to others. This is vital to my relationship with other Christian men but absolutely required in my relationship with non-Christians. I believe there is no greater witness than encouraging someone who is lost, in words, backed up with deeds.

Binding together with brothers in Christ is vital to ourselves and to each other.
- We're in this together.

There are many people surrounding you daily who are dealing with issues that need your attention:
- Lift them up.

Encouraging others is not something you do sporadically but should be a part of your daily life.
- Give us this day our daily….

Encouragement should not be superficial, but should have the depth of getting to know those around you so that you see their issues and concerns
- The Pledge

Are you so in tune with others' needs and committed to helping them that you could be nicknamed "Mr. Encouragement"?
- What's in a name?

Challenge:
Men: You have an opportunity to be the greatest encourager in the world to your young men; my father is my hero in this aspect for me. Teach them though your example.
Young Men: You come into contact with so many people daily, at school, during your activities. Learn to look outside yourself and make it a habit to encourage those around you.

Encouragement – Gotta Have Some

Monday

Verse: Hebrews 10:24-25

> *And let us consider how we may spur one another on toward love and good deeds. Let us not give up meeting together, as some are in the habit of doing, but let us encourage one another—and all the more as you see the Day approaching.*

Father's Thoughts: We are not in this alone. God has given you Christian brothers and sisters for a reason. The time has come or will come soon when you will leave for college or for work or to get married. You will have choices to make of when and where (and if) to worship, join a Bible study and surround yourself with other believers.

Sons' Thoughts: Teamwork. It is the factor that can cause one team to outdo the other. One of the biggest parts of teamwork is encouraging one another. We should not practice this only on the playing field, but also in our walk with other Christians.

Discussion Questions: Are you ready to commit to seek out other believers wherever you go, to encourage, and be encouraged by the fellowship? If you are in a Sunday School class or other small group, do you work together as a team to encourage each other?

Notes: _____
_____
_____
_____

Tuesday

Verse: Isaiah 1:17

Learn to do right! Seek justice, encourage the oppressed. Defend the cause of the fatherless, plead the case of the widow.

Father's Thoughts: Now matter how bad you are feeling about yourself, maybe something at school, at home or with friends is not going like you want it to, there is ALWAYS someone else who is in worse shape than you. It could be the kid that just had a death in the family, one whose dad or mom lost a job. It could be a divorce situation; it could be someone who is truly poor and struggling. We as Christian men are called to DO RIGHT. We are to stand up and encourage those who are hurting with both our actions and our words.

Sons' Thoughts: As humans, we are given the knowledge to know the difference between right and wrong. This verse is simply stating to act upon it.

Discussion Questions: Who do you know who is hurting? What can you do today to encourage that person?

Notes: _____
_____
_____
_____

Wednesday

Verse: Hebrews 3:13

> *But encourage one another daily, as long as it is called Today, so that none of you may be hardened by sin's deceitfulness.*

Father's Thoughts: We are called to pray without ceasing. That is our communication with God. We are also called to encourage without ceasing; this is our communication with man. Don't underestimate the power of a kind word.

Sons' Thoughts: Encouragement is one of the biggest tools we have to reach out to people. People will be keener to listen if they constantly hear uplifting things come out of our mouths.

Discussion Questions: I know you sit in your room just before you go to bed, making that last phone call, sending that last text message. Is it just talk? Can you find a way to turn these communications into encouragement?

Notes: _____
_____
_____
_____

Thursday

Verse: 2 Timothy 4:2

> *Preach the Word; be prepared in season and out of season; correct, rebuke and encourage—with great patience and careful instruction.*

Father's Thoughts: When we have an opportunity to encourage someone there are a few keys we need to remember. Don't just give superficial encouragement 'have a good day' or 'I'm pulling for you.' Your encouragement should have depth, it should be from God's word. Encouragement will and should involve risk. We should give it even when someone may not be receptive.

Sons' Thoughts: We always need to be prepared. Someone could come to us looking for help when we least expect it. Always stay on your guard for God to open up an opportunity.

Discussion Questions: Are you willing to do the hard work and have the patience to be a great encourager for the Lord?

Notes: _____
_____
_____
_____

Friday

Verse: Acts 4:36-37

> *Joseph, a Levite from Cyprus, whom the apostles called Barnabas (which means Son of Encouragement), sold a field he owned and brought the money and put it at the apostles' feet.*

Father's Thoughts: Encouragement can come through actions, not just words. Joseph was an active encourager. He was not flashy, yet he lived a life that was so visible that they gave him a nickname about it. It is an old phrase but 'let your actions speak louder than words.'

Sons' Thoughts: Do you show others your beliefs also through your actions? Many times this can be a better encourager than any spoken word.

Discussion Questions: There are going to be a lot of friends around you that need encouragement. What can you DO rather than SAY to lift them up?

Notes: _____

_____
_____
_____

Week 15

Relationships of a Godly Youth

—⚞—

Let me say this first, being a Godly Youth does not mean perfection. None of us, young or old, can bear that burden of expectation. The key of being a Godly Youth is being different, set apart for God's service, trying and striving to do what is right in the eyes of the Lord and gaining the respect of those around you. Much of how you are perceived by others is how you treat others, starting at home. This is not all about your relationship with your parents but extends to your siblings as well. People will look at how you act towards your immediate family and, right or wrong, will judge you by what they see and hear. [I will take time to brag on one of my kids. After the oldest went off to college I overheard one of the younger son's friends saying how glad he was to have his older sibling out of the house. My son, though he may have been tempted to parrot the other boy, disagreed and told him how great and cool his brother was and that he would really miss him. That spoke volumes to me and to others listening about the positive relationship the two of them had]. Look at how you treat others around you. I know I am not the best example as my boys will tell you. But no matter how old or young we are, we should start with relationships in building our witness for Christ.

The buck stops…..at home
- Honor, obey and live.

Look to the qualities of leading by example, even when you are young.
- People are looking, already.

How do young men treat other men?
- R.E.S.P.E.C.T.

How do young men treat women?
- R.E.S.P.E.C.T. Act II

You can still be young….and spiritually mature.
- Time to grow up.

Challenge:
Men: Teach your young men to respect relationships with others, starting at home and then permeating all their interactions.
Young Men: Start now learning how to build relationships with all those around you. Apply your relationship with Christ to your relationships to all, young/old, male/female, family/stranger.

Relationships of a Godly Youth

Monday

Verse: Ephesians 6:1-3

> *Children, obey your parents in the Lord, for this is right. "Honor your father and mother" —which is the first commandment with a promise—"that it may go well with you and that you may enjoy long life on the earth"*

Father's Thoughts: Enough said……..if you don't obey your parents they might just take you out? Okay, that's easy and self-serving for a parent to say, but what about those with parents who are not particularly honorable? This is where there will be a real separation of young men that have turned their lives over to Christ. It is the ability to work with your parents even in areas where you do not agree or in areas where they may be leading you down the wrong path. Honor them with your love, pray for them and do your best to talk through situations that might be difficult, obey them in the little things and earn their trust.

Sons' Thoughts: Obeying your parents = long life. Hey! That's good enough for me!

Discussion Questions: What are some practical ways fathers and sons can work together to create and build positive relationships? What is the best part of your relationship with your parents, the part that makes you want to obey? Can you find a way to emphasize that part daily?

Notes: _____
_____
_____
_____

Tuesday

Verse: 1 Timothy 4:12

> *Don't let anyone look down on you because you are young, but set an example for the believers in speech, in life, in love, in faith and in purity.*

Father's Thoughts: Youth can be a gift and a burden. Even 'good kids' can get labeled with a broad brush when adults talk about the problems of today's generation. So how do you combat these generalizations? Paul gave young Timothy the key—set an example. Don't be afraid to do the right thing, to love, to live, to abstain, to speak in positive words, not those that tear down.

Sons' Thoughts: I've found this verse popping into my head a lot recently. I think with this generation a stereotype is put on teenagers, and the movies aren't helping. We need to look past this and show the older folks that kids these days actually do have morals and beliefs that they can stick to.

Discussion Questions: Are you willing to stand up and be the example of a Godly Youth?

Notes: _____
_____
_____
_____

Wednesday

Verse: 1 Timothy 5:1

> *Do not rebuke an older man harshly, but exhort him as if he were your father. Treat younger men as brothers,*

Father's Thoughts: You do not have to be old to be a leader. If you are capable and willing, you can rise to levels of leadership at a young age. Military officers, entrepreneurs, and college student body officers are several examples of young leaders. How you execute that leadership is important, and the most important part is knowing how to treat people. You should always show proper respect, especially to those older than yourself.

Sons' Thoughts: Treat others as they should be treated. Don't judge someone because of their age.

Discussion Questions: Has God given you leadership qualities as a young man? How have you used your opportunities to lead?

Notes: _____
_____
_____
_____

Thursday

Verse: 1 Timothy 5:2

> *[Treat] older women as mothers, and younger women as sisters, with absolute purity.*

Father's Thoughts: Whether we know it or not, people judge us by how we treat other people. When we have an opportunity to interact with women, do we respect them? Do we treat them with love and with grace? When we deal with younger women do we put them through a filter of what they look like, what they can do for us? We need to treat them as family, as current or potential sisters in Christ. As young men, I know this is tough. You are sexual beings looking and longing for that perfect partner which God has made for you. Until you find her, can you respect and treat all women as you would your mother or sister?

Sons' Thoughts: Women deserve to be treated like women. Not as prizes or just a body. We all fall into temptations of lust. Think about it this way. When you find yourself in lust, think about how you would feel if you heard someone lusting after your own mother or sister.

Discussion Questions: While you are waiting to find your mate for life, can you respect and treat all women as you would your mother or sister?

Notes: _____
_____
_____
_____

Friday

Verse: 1 Colossians 13:11

> *When I was a child, I talked like a child, I thought like a child, I reasoned like a child. When I became a man, I put childish ways behind me.*

Father's Thoughts: Have you ever gotten mad because you thought someone was treating you like a baby? Maybe they insisted on doing something for you that you could do yourself, or would not let you do something difficult because they said you were too young. Well, you are physically growing but maturity is not just how big you are, but how responsible you become. Sometimes Christians can get stuck in spiritual childhood. God cannot treat them as adults because they do not display the maturity to take on responsibility or risks.

Sons' Thoughts: Maturity gains respect. You can't obtain someone's respect if you still have temper tantrums at a sales meeting.

Discussion Questions: What are you doing to grow mature spiritually? Can God trust you to become a spiritual man, or will you be stuck, treated forever as a child?

Notes: _____
_____
_____
_____

Week 16

Good Deeds for the Do-Gooder

"Do as I say, not as I do". How often we hear from sources around us "help others, help the poor, be concerned about the hungry, feed the children," yet when you confront the source they often say something like, "Oh, it is my calling to point out the problems, not to solve them." It is really very simple. We need to put legs to our religion and that means now and often. If you just open your eyes and look around, you will see people with needs that if left unchecked will starve them, emotionally, physically and spiritually. This is a call to action. As a young man you have an opportunity to begin a life pattern of openly supporting those in need.

It starts with a vision, your own. I mean open your eyes and open your heart to see what needs are out there. It means applying your spiritual gifts (God-given skills and desires) to meet the needs of others. If requires you to give of yourself, your time, your money (we will talk about that another time), your muscle. If you belong to a church, search out a mission trip, not an inward camp-like experience, although they can be beneficial, but a real mission trip where you will roll up your sleeves and help someone whose needs are greater than yours. Also, search out others who also want to help others. This will be a situation where groupthink can change lives.

'Religion', especially when referring to Christianity, is often given a bad name.
- Religion defined

Say………..and do.
- Truth in advertising

Which is more important:
- Faith or Deeds?

You will leave a legacy…. what do you want yours to be.
- How will you be remembered?

It pays to surround yourself with like-minded friends – well, what about your girlfriends?
- Want some help?

Challenge:
Men: If helping others is not a part of your life, this is a great time to lead by example. Take the time to schedule specific projects with your young man so that you can learn to serve others together.
Young Men: Make serving others a basic part of your life, and begin now. Learn to back up works with deeds and make good deeds a part of all aspects of your life. Surround yourself with others, including those you date, who will share a servant's heart.

Good Deeds for the Do-Gooder

Monday

Verse: James 1:27

> *Religion that God our Father accepts as pure and faultless is this: to look after orphans and widows in their distress and to keep one-self from being polluted by the world.*

Father's Thoughts: Christianity is all about our relationship with the living God. Religion is how we display that relationship to the world. James, the earthly brother of Jesus gives us a practical lesson. God wants you to display your relationship with Him in outward form by helping others and by setting a good example for others through self- control.

Sons' Thoughts: Many times we might ask ourselves "God has given us so much, what can we ever give in return?" Well, there's your answer.

Discussion Questions: Why are so many people down on "religion". Could it be because we are not doing these two things that God accepts as pure and faultless?

Notes: _____
_____
_____
_____

Tuesday

Verse: James 2:15-16

> *Suppose a brother or sister is without clothes and daily food. If one of you says to him, "Go, I wish you well; keep warm and well fed," but does nothing about his physical needs, what good is it?*

Father's Thoughts: Put legs to your religion. Isn't this what James is saying? You have heard that actions speak louder than words so it is time to put in some action. Every day you are surrounded with people who have needs. If you only give them a pep talk it will not do much to meet that need. You may not see other guys at school that don't have clothes or don't have enough to eat, but they still have needs that are holding them back. You can be a part of meeting those needs, but it will take more than a casual phrase. You have to do something.

Sons' Thoughts: This verse is explaining the fact that actions speak louder than words. If you tell someone you're praying for them and never do it, that's worse than not even saying anything.

Discussion Questions: What do you think the greatest need is among your friends at school? What can you do in a practical sense to meet their needs?

Notes: _____
_____
_____
_____

Wednesday

Verse: James 2:17-18

> *In the same way, faith by itself, if it is not accompanied by action, is dead. But someone will say, "You have faith; I have deeds." Show me your faith without deeds, and I will show you my faith by what I do.*

Father's Thoughts: There is a modern phrase, 'do as I say, not as I do.' But James, Jesus' earthly brother got it right by saying, 'do as I do'. I hope that I can be an example to you as someone who works for God with my hands, my money, my time. Challenge me in this as I will challenge you.

Sons' Thoughts: If we don't act on our faith, what good is it doing? Most of the time, people should see our faith through our actions.

Discussion Questions: What "deeds" can we do together as father and sons? Who can we help, who can we pray for, who can we encourage together?

Notes: _____
_____
_____
_____

Thursday

Verse: Proverbs 14:21

He who despises his neighbor sins, but blessed is he who is kind to the needy.

Father's Thoughts: Practical love is putting legs to our faith. Withholding that love for any reason is a sin. Solomon understood that putting action into love is a blessing for both sides. The practical side of our faith, clothed in good works, will bring much more real blessing to our own lives as we help others.

Sons' Thoughts: I know when I read this verse, I think about the annoying kids I used to live down the street from. But I think this verse is talking about everyone around us as neighbors, and we should treat them all as if they were ourselves.

Discussion Questions: Who is the neighbor you need to stop despising and start showing love and kindness?

Notes: _____
_____
_____

Friday

Verse: Proverbs 31:20

> *She opens her arms to the poor and extends her hands to the needy.*

Father's Thoughts: What is a partnership? Can partners go in opposite directions and meet their goals? This will be so very important in marriage. If you have made a commitment to helping others, make sure that those you date and the one you eventually marry have the same heart.

Sons' Thoughts: You always have to be careful about the girls you become interested in. If you go out with them, how will they affect you as a person? Will they bring out your good qualities, or make you act like someone else? Try to find a girl who shares your beliefs and won't pressure you to change.

Discussion Questions: How do or will you judge those you date? Will it be by external beauty only, or will you seek a helpmate that has a heart for God's works?

Notes: _____
_____
_____
_____

Week 17

Hard Work – Sweating It Out

Work, it's the curse of the working class, right? Work is a part of life and a part of being a man. As men, we are expected to provide for ourselves and our families and that means developing skills in a specific area, be it a physical skill, business skill, relationship skill, or any talent that can be turned into a profession. Once you have developed these skills and talents then attitude and focus take over. No matter what we do, no matter what financial reward it brings us, we should dedicate that part of our lives to the Lord. God expects us to take a healthy pride in what we do and to do it for Him, not for man.

Some Christians struggle with the definitional boundaries of secular work and ministry. This should not be a struggle because for many if not most of us our work is our ministry. Work inevitably means contact with other people. These can be co-workers, clients, vendors, etc. that you see every day and with whom you will have an opportunity to share the news of Jesus Christ. Maybe you will become a full- time worker for Christ, a minister, a missionary, an evangelist. These callings also require hard, dedicated work.

Look at those working around you. Do you have respect for them and what they do, the way they use their skills to touch lives? Make a point to look at the work others are doing and respect the values of hard work and the benefits of working as unto the Lord.

Paul knew what hard work was all about.
- Don't be a burden.

Look at those working around you, for you. What examples do they display?
- Hard- working heroes

Are you working for yourself or for someone greater?
- Who's the boss?

Everyone has one, right?
- Serving it up

Oops, the shoe is on the other foot.
- When you are the boss?

Challenge:
Men: Talk to your young men about your career choices. Explore ways that you have learned to bring your Christian walk into your workplace.

Young Men: Think about how you will choose a career that will not only bless you but also those around you. Dedicate yourself to work hard and to respect those working around you.

Hard Work – Sweating It Out

Monday

Verse: 1 Thessalonians 5:2:9

> *Surely you remember, brothers, our toil and hardship; we worked night and day in order not to be a burden to anyone while we preached the gospel of God to you.*

Father's Thoughts: Paul could have asked that he be compensated for his preaching. He was giving them the words of life. Surely he was entitled to room and board! Instead, he used the skills he had, tent making, working all day and then preaching at night, to fund his mission. It was his investment. Yes, Paul was called to preach but there were times he was called to be a preacher/businessman.

Sons' Thoughts: Everyone has a passion for something, some kind of hobby. But we have to be careful not to spend too much time on these things and keep focused on God.

Discussion Questions: What are some ways you can you mix your desired profession with the work of the Lord?

Notes: _____
_____
_____
_____

Tuesday

Verse: 1 Thessalonians 5:12-13

> *Now we ask you, brothers, to respect those who work hard among you, who are over you in the Lord and who admonish you. Hold them in the highest regard in love because of their work.*

Father's Thoughts: If we are working hard for the Lord's purposes, we should not be constantly looking for praise. But that does not mean it isn't nice to get some if you are not expecting it. We should encourage those that work hard around us and for us.

Sons' Thoughts: To be honest I don't love all of my teachers that I have in school, and I'm sure many of you feel the same. But that shouldn't stop us from respecting them and the time they put in to helping us.

Discussion Questions: When was the last time that you thanked your Sunday School teacher, or your small group leader, even your pastor, for all the hours they have put into their work? When was the last time you thanked your teachers, your coaches, your parents?

Notes: _____
_____
_____
_____

Wednesday

Verse: Colossians 3:23

Whatever you do, work at it with all your heart, as working for the Lord, not for men.

Father's Thoughts: There is no greater curse in pro sports than to be labeled as someone who had untapped potential but lacked a work ethic. Those careers are usually short lived. Sometimes the boss is a pain, and the work boring. Getting past that, you need to realize that God is watching, whether or not other men are taking notice. Surprise that boss, surprise that teacher, surprise that coach by displaying your full talent and effort for God.

Sons' Thoughts: As I've learned from past experiences, teachers and coaches will always prefer a kid who works hard over someone smarter and more talented who slacks off. So whenever you feel like you've done sufficient work, push a little bit harder and represent the Kingdom.

Discussion Questions: What is one thing that you can commit to do better today because you are going to dedicate your work to the Lord?

Notes: _____
_____
_____
_____

Thursday

Verse: Ephesians 6:5

> *Slaves, obey your earthly masters with respect and fear and with sincerity of heart, just as you would obey Christ.*

Father's Thoughts: I heard once that there was a poll that found that 79% of people were not happy at work. Well, maybe as Christians we just have to get over it. Hey, it's the same with school and your teachers. How many times do you find yourself talking down your teachers, administrators, and principals - even better targets - vice-principals. Respect is always the first step. They are there for a reason and have skills and experience that should be acknowledged and 'feared.' Maybe they find you just as difficult to deal with.

Sons' Thoughts: Although the 13th amendment (don't quote me on that) abandoned slavery, we still have people we must obey. As much as we might not like it, we should have the utmost respect for our parents and obey what they say.

Discussion Questions: What is one step that you can take, with all sincerity, to build a better relationship with the authority figures in your life?

Notes: _____
_____
_____
_____

Friday

Verse: Colossians 4:1

> *Masters, provide your slaves with what is right and fair, because you know that you also have a Master in heaven.*

Father's Thoughts: Okay, now you are not the worker, you're the boss. Remember all those teachers, coaches and bosses that you criticized? Turn it all around, now it's you! What do you think people will say about you behind your back?

Sons' Thoughts: And someday, all of us might have the chance to become parents or bosses. We need to take the respect we had for our authorities and transfer it to those who are now following our lead.

Discussion Questions: When you are a boss, will you be accused of being fair and doing what is right? Will they be right?

Notes: _____
_____
_____
_____

Week 18

Greed and Money – It's Not Just the Fat Cats

—m—

Why do you think that Jesus chose to talk about money more than any single topic during His earthly ministry? Since God created man, he knows our every weakness, and besides women, our greatest weaknesses are the things that possess us. That's right, they tend to possess us rather than the other way around. As men we tend to love our stuff and hold it up to the world to tell everyone, 'Hey, look at me, I have the best ….., I just bought the newest ……" Somehow, some way we have to gain the upper hand; we have to let go of the stuff and give it to God.

Right up front, Christian men, young and old need to determine how they are going to treat money and possessions. It does not matter where you are starting, rich/poor, inner city/suburban, young/old, you must ask yourself, "How am I going to treat the assets and resources that I possess, will posses, want to possess?" Desiring financial gain is NOT a sin. We have numerous examples of "rich guys" in the Bible. We see how God has blessed individuals and countries over history, but we also see examples of where men have let their money, fame and fortune ruin their lives. What turns into sin is putting those possessions before God and letting the love of money, the love of the pursuit of money or the misuse of money gain the upper hand and control our heart, mind and soul, the things that God desires for himself.

What is going to control you?
- Making the tough choice

Are we really the sum of all our stuff?
- He who has the most toys....

Who are we serving? Are we leading by example?
- What is stewardship?

What is this 'tithing' thing all about?
- Whose money is it anyway?

What is the true gift from God?
- Contentment

Challenge:
Men: By example and by word, teach your young men to be good managers of money. Show them how a godly man approaches money and possessions.

Young Men: Begin early to determine your approach to wealth and money. Start young to have healthy money management habits and be stewards of what you will possess.

Greed and Money – It's Not Just the Fat Cats

Monday

Verse: Matthew 6:24

> *"No one can serve two masters. Either he will hate the one and love the other, or he will be devoted to the one and despise the other. You cannot serve both God and Money.*

Father's Thoughts: Money is a vicious master. Ask anyone with a mortgage or credit cards. Money and the pursuit of it can so consume you that you can forget about anything else. It can be as powerful a drug as heroin or cocaine. I have heard that more arguments in a marriage are over money than all other subjects combined. So how do you handle it? By giving it to God. Simple answer, but as weak men, hard to do.

Sons' Thoughts: This verse simply challenges us to make a choice. Are we going to follow God, or become consumed in the worldly things we long for?

Discussion Questions: How can you begin to have a healthy attitude about money and possessions as a young man that will help you avoid 'slavery' as you get older?

Notes: _____
_____
_____
_____

Tuesday

Verse: Luke 12:15

> *Then [Jesus] said to [his disciples], "Watch out! Be on your guard against all kinds of greed; a man's life does not consist in the abundance of possessions."*

Father's Thoughts: The purpose of life is so much more than having a lot of Man Toys. It will be a constant temptation all of your life to be defined by your possessions. It can be fun to be recognized as the guy with the hot car, the one with the great video games, biggest house, and the most spending money. Jesus knew that our possessions could end up possessing us.

Sons' Thoughts: We all want to stand out. But try doing it in the safe way-by standing out for your beliefs and your caring personality, not by having the newest iPod or cell phone. Because if we spend too much time trying to get those things, they could eventually get us.

Discussion Questions: What are those things in your life that are your prized possessions? How can you turn those from being obsessions into being secondary in your life, second to your relationship with God and man?

Notes: _____
_____
_____
_____

Wednesday

Verse: 1 Peter 5:2-3

> *Be shepherds of God's flock that is under your care, serving as overseers—not because you must, but because you are willing, as God wants you to be; not greedy for money, but eager to serve; not lording it over those entrusted to you, but being examples to the flock.*

Father's Thoughts: Each of us is called to be shepherds of God's little lambs. Peter of all people learned this the hard way. Our flock may be as small as our immediate family or it may be as large as a nation. What can keep us from serving that flock well? The world is littered with men who lost their way, lost their flock due to greed. Making money became the most important thing in their lives and they forgot how to give.

Sons' Thoughts: As Christians, we are called to be examples of Christ. Not bragging about how great we are, but showing people how to become followers of the one true God.

Discussion Questions: What role do money and possessions play in your life? Be honest and assess how this might be a problem later in life.

Notes: _____
_____
_____
_____

Thursday

Verse: 1 Corinthians 16:2-3

On the first day of every week, each one of you should set aside a sum of money in keeping with his income, saving it up, so that when I come no collections will have to be made. Then, when I arrive, I will give letters of introduction to the men you approve and send them with your gift to Jerusalem.

Father's Thoughts: Priorities. Paul knew that it would be hard to make giving a priority, so he made it simple. Put aside what you are giving to the Lord first. Let giving be the initial action, not an afterthought. Then when the need arises there is not a scramble for funds, it is there waiting. It takes faith, determination and discipline.

Sons' Thoughts: My advice to all of you. I've tried to learn good money habits early in my life. It is so important to learn it so when the time comes to start managing your money, it will be a habit that you are already used to.

Discussion Questions: Are you learning good money management habits? Have I been a good example?

Notes: _____
_____
_____
_____

Friday

Verse: Ecclesiastes 5:19-20

> *Moreover, when God gives any man wealth and possessions, and enables him to enjoy them, to accept his lot and be happy in his work—this is a gift of God.*

Father's Thoughts: Men have such trouble with contentment. We are always striving for more: more money, more power, more stuff. Maybe it's because we don't recognize the source of our wealth and possessions. They are from God and he has given them to us because he loves us and wants us to enjoy life and living.

Sons' Thoughts: All the time we see our success as our own doing. Rarely do we sit down and thank God for all that he gives us. But our success comes from him and him alone.

Discussion Questions: Can you take a few minutes each day and thank God for what you have; before you ask Him for what you think you want or need?

Notes: _____
_____
_____
_____

Week 19

When I Run, I Feel God's Pleasure

Running is such a great metaphor for our Christian life and I am grateful to Paul for giving us so many great verses paralleling the two. In the 70's – my teenage years – the great JOGGING phase hit and many, many people began to run. It was the age of Nike, Steve Prefontaine, Jim Ryun, Dr. Kenneth Cooper and Jim Fixx. Everybody was running, it was a national pastime worthy of note in Forrest Gump. However, like most fads, it began to fad(e) away. All those pairs of shoes began to collect dust in the closet next to the clothes that used to fit when we were actually running and exercising. The discipline faded, the tight abs replaced with a sizable gut and knee/hip replacement surgery.

Discipline, that is what came and went with the latest whim. It was just too much hard work and well, we had so much to do, families to raise, careers to chase. The discipline of a fulfilling Christian life, like running, takes hard work, discipline and dedication. While busy-ness surrounds us, we have to take the time to study, pray and get involved in saving souls. Watching the dedication and hard work of my oldest son as a distance runner has given me new appreciation for what it takes to run competitively. The race for a meaningful life in Christ takes no less sacrifice.

- Don't stop now.
    o Running the race of life with perseverance

- I got a really big medal.
  - Running to win the prize

- No Pain, No Gain
  - Doing what you have trained to do

- Today's Pain, Tomorrow's Glory
  - To the prepared go the spoils

- What are you really training for?
  - Focusing on the right goal

Challenge:

Men: Many of you participated in sports and you enjoy watching your sons compete and sometimes excel in sports and other activities. As they participate in sports or other activities, share with them the lessons that can be learned, lessons that Paul and others shared.

Young Men: Whether or not you are an athlete, learn to approach your Christian walk as a top athlete approaches his sport, through discipline, training and focus.

When I Run, I Feel God's Pleasure

Monday

Verse: Hebrews 12:1-2

> *Therefore, since we are surrounded by such a great cloud of witnesses, let us throw off everything that hinders and the sin that so easily entangles, and let us run with perseverance the race marked out for us. Let us fix our eyes on Jesus, the author and perfecter of our faith, who for the joy set before him endured the cross, scorning its shame, and sat down at the right hand of the throne of God.*

Father's Thoughts: Endurance is the mark of a great distance runner. But if you tried to run with extra weight tied on to you, you would quickly break down. Don't let sin be an anchor. Also, when you run a race, you have to stay on the course, follow the markers, follow the trail. Christ has set that trail out before us, he has given us his word as a guide. While we endure the race, he endured the cross so that our race has a purpose, a destination, a finish line.

Sons' Thoughts: I am one who knows exactly what he is talking about. I have been a distance runner for over six years now and have run my share of races. When running a race, there is only one thing that you can focus on, and that is the race itself. It took me a good four years to perfect this, and when I did, I made a huge breakthrough, running much faster than I ever had before. When I first started racing, I would always be singing a song in my head or doing something to distract from the pain. Now though, no matter how long the race is, I have learned to focus on nothing but the race, how I feel, where I am supposed to be, etc. It is exactly as Paul states here. You have to forget everything else that is going on, or you won't be able to run a strong spiritual race.

Discussion Questions: Are you letting anything weight you down, take you off the course, break down your endurance?

Notes: _____
_____
_____
_____

Tuesday

Verse: 1 Corinthians 9:24

> *Do you not know that in a race all the runners run, but only one gets the prize? Run in such a way as to get the prize.*

Father's Thoughts: Focus on the goal, be willing to sacrifice, be willing to endure pain in order to win. This is the requirement of a runner. Would Paul have used such an example if he did not believe we must do the same in our Christian commitment? In a race there are no short cuts, there are no quick roads to glory. It is the way you train, the way you stretch yourself that determines your success. Christ expects no less of us as we serve Him.

Sons' Thoughts: In many races, I know that I am not going to finish in first place. It is something that I have grown accustomed to over the past two years, as I have had two of the top distance runners in the nation on my team. That fact, though, never stopped me from going out there and running my best. Even though I knew I probably wouldn't win, I didn't give up all hope before the race started. I ran as if I was trying to win and that is what makes all of the difference.

Discussion Questions: What are some things you have been doing lately to train and prepare to serve God? Have you stretched yourself?

Notes: _____
_____
_____
_____

Wednesday

Verse: 1 Corinthians 9:25-27

> *Everyone who competes in the games goes into strict training. They do it to get a crown that will not last; but we do it to get a crown that will last forever. Therefore I do not run like a man running aimlessly; I do not fight like a man beating the air. No, I beat my body and make it my slave so that after I have preached to others, I myself will not be disqualified for the prize.*

Father's Thoughts: Self-discipline is one of the hardest things to accomplish. Often we look to do the right thing but for the wrong motive, or our heart is in the right place but we get lazy. Just like the runner who has a detailed plan, we should have a disciplined approach to our Christian walk. We should set out goals for ourselves, goals in the area of missions or ministries we get involved in, goal for giving, goals for overcoming spiritual obstacles. God gave us minds and bodies that we should always use to His glory.

Sons' Thoughts: Again, I know what it is like to make my body a slave to my mind. I sometimes have to trick my mind into going always harder and faster, and enduring more pain. I do not let my body give in to the pain and break stride. The same should be said for a spiritual race. It will undoubtedly be hard, painful, and grueling. This means that we can not let ourselves break form, for then the race will become much tougher.

Discussion Questions: What are some ways that you can plan out your spiritual walk? Do you keep a journal to follow your progress? Can you work with a mentor or other Christian brother to "train" together?

Notes: _____
_____
_____
_____

Thursday

Verse: Hebrews 12:11-13

> *No discipline seems pleasant at the time, but painful. Later on, however, it produces a harvest of righteousness and peace for those who have been trained by it. Therefore, strengthen your feeble arms and weak knees. "Make level paths for your feet," so that the lame may not be disabled, but rather healed.*

Father's Thoughts: Practice, practice, practice. I see you roll your eyes when I ask, "Did you have a good practice?" or "How was your run today?" It hurts, but the discipline to practice hard pays off in the long run (no pun intended). We may not think that our study of the scriptures, our discipline of prayer, our discipline of giving, or the pain of trials will pay off. As we strengthen our spiritual muscles, we get ourselves ready for that day we are called to run the race of a lifetime, to do great things.

Sons' Thoughts: One thing that I absolutely hate to do is work out my upper body. I would much rather go for a ten-mile run than spend ten minutes in the weight room, but I know that it will make be a better athlete and that it will eventually pay off. I know what it is like when you just don't want to spend time reading the Bible or going to church, but it will pay off, even in ways that you don't expect.

Discussion Questions: Are you ready? Have you put in your spiritual practice time?

Notes: _____
_____
_____
_____

Friday

Verse: 1 Timothy 4:7-8

> *Have nothing to do with godless myths and old wives' tales; rather, train yourself to be godly. For physical training is of some value, but godliness has value for all things, holding promise for both the present life and the life to come.*

Father's Thoughts: We can really get caught up in things of this world that can take our eyes off God's purpose for our lives. Too many times we get caught up in the pettiness of the "entertainment" industry and spend more time on temporary things than we do on the eternal. Spiritual training leads to Godliness so each of us has to ask how much time we spend in training. I believe it takes more than one or two hours on Sunday.

Sons' Thoughts: This is a verse that I need to remind myself that while I want to be a good athlete, it is really not that important. It is of some value, but godliness has value for all things. Athletics should not completely take over your life, or you will not be fulfilled.

Discussion Questions: Do you have "training" time during the week? Are you dedicated to setting aside time to be truly training for a godly lifestyle? What kind of training do you think will work best for you?

Notes: _____
_____
_____
_____

Week 20

Salvation – And the Truth Shall Set You Free

—⚏—

The other day my oldest son and his college teammates were heroes. They had just left a track meet in Johnson City, Tennessee and were heading back to school when they had an opportunity to do what many of us dream about, save a life. Here were the text messages we exchanged:

- Son, 9:20pm "we just saved a house from burning. We saw it off the interstate and stopped and ran in to check if anyone was inside"
- Dad, 9:20pm "Wow, where was this, on 81? Was everyone okay?"
- Son, 9:22pm "Yeah, there were only two puppies inside and the shed was gone."
- Dad, 9:23pm "Well good job, are the firemen there yet?"
- Son, 9:25pm "Yeah, I think everyone in East Tennessee was there."
- Dad, 9:26pm "Well I assume u saved the puppies. What about the owners, did they show up?"
- Son, 9:27pm "No, they were not there yet"

It seems like such a simple act but as a father, the unselfish act of these young men running across a field in order to save lives (albeit puppies, they didn't know, there could have been children in there) at their own risk made me so very proud of them. What a vision of the selfless act that Christ performed on the cross. He runs to us at full speed to save us from sin and destruction, to bring us safely home to God our Father.

- Yep, I blew it.
    o Understand that we all have sinned.

- Jesus Paid it All
    o Christ died for our sins.

- One- way street
    o Christ points the way.

- There really is a point.
    o Salvation through Christ has a future.

- Celebrate, Celebrate!
    o God rejoices when you accept him and come home.

Challenge:

Men: Discuss the basics of salvation with your young man. Take the time to discuss the blessings of a relationship with God through Christ.

Young Men: Have you come to the point of trusting in Christ for your salvation? Discuss this with your Dad and start a journey with God today.

Salvation – And the Truth Shall Set You Free

Monday

Verse: Luke 15:21

> *"The son said to him, 'Father, I have sinned against heaven and against you. I am no longer worth to be called your son.'"*

Father's Thoughts: We have to come to a point where we really understand what is at stake, what we have done to separate ourselves from God. Confession must be pure and passionate. This son had to hit the lowest of lows before he was compelled to come back to his father. If we do not have to wait that long, we would be so much better off.

Sons' Thoughts: Remorse is something that we will have to deal with. There will always be something in life that we will regret. And when we do, we should go to full measures to make it right with whomever we hurt.

Discussion Questions: Have you truly hit a point where you are both aware of your sins and the impact that sin has on your relationship to God and to others? Have you come to a point where you are ready to completely and sincerely ask for God's forgiveness?

Notes: _____
_____
_____
_____

Tuesday

Verse: Galatians 3:13

> *Christ redeemed us from the curse of the law by becoming a curse for us, for it is written: "Cursed is everyone who is hung on a tree."*

Father's Thoughts: This is one of the hardest concepts to grasp in my Christian walk that Jesus took on our sins in order to spare us from death. In modern terms, he has our back. He loves us that much that he would step in front of the bullet, take the hit, become our blocking fullback.

Sons' Thoughts: Christ went through a lot to save us, even to the point of becoming cursed himself.

Discussion Questions: Why did a sacrifice have to be made to make salvation work?

Notes: _____
_____
_____
_____

Wednesday

Verse: Romans 5:1

> *Therefore, since we have been justified through faith, we have peace with God through our Lord Jesus Christ,*

Father's Thoughts: Salvation through faith leads to peace. Why? Well, think about what life would be like if you had to justify yourself by your own actions. You would worry constantly about whether or not what you were doing to earn salvation was good enough, fast enough, worthy enough. No, Christ died for us. He did the work. He paid the price so that we receive this gift through Him, not by our own actions.

Sons' Thoughts: That is, in essence, what Christianity is all about, being at peace with God. God wants us to be in perfect harmony with him, but it is impossible because of our sinful nature.

Discussion Questions: Can you accept justification and live in the peace that it brings?

Notes: _____
_____
_____
_____

Thursday

Verse: Romans 6:4

> *We were therefore buried with him through baptism into death in order that, just as Christ was raised from the dead through the glory of the Father, we too may live a new life.*

Father's Thoughts: John may or may not have been the first to use the act of baptism in his call for the people of Israel to repent. But with Christ's confirmation of this activity with the subsequent pleasure of his Father, this has become an outward symbol of our inward salvation.

Sons' Thoughts: Baptism is an extremely strong visual cue to show us exactly what we are doing when we accept Christ into our lives. We are washed away of all our sins, and are raised as a different person.

Discussion Questions: Why do you think the symbolism of baptism was given to us by Christ? What importance do you think we should put on public baptism in the church?

Notes: _____
_____
_____
_____

Friday

Verse: Luke 15:24

> *"For this son of mine was dead and is alive again; he was lost and is found." So they began to celebrate.*

Father's Thoughts: I have been traveling now for the last six months. I have to leave the house on Monday and do not get back until Friday afternoon. Around noon on Thursdays, I begin to get a big grin on my face. I get to go home soon. I will soon get to hug my wife, son and daughter. I begin to celebrate. The whole five-hour drive back I celebrate that I get to spend time with my family. The same thing happened last Monday; I took a side trip and had a birthday dinner with our oldest son who is away at college. The whole way there I celebrated, "I get to see my son again." Maybe in some small way, I got to feel what God feels when he is spiritually reunited with a lost child who accepts His salvation and comes home.

Sons' Thoughts: Of course a father would celebrate if he thought that his son was dead only to find out that he was actually alive. This is what God does when we decide to start a relationship with him.

Discussion Questions: What is God's reaction to our salvation? What should be our reaction when someone comes to know Christ?

Notes: _____
_____
_____
_____

Week 21

Salvation – Taking the Road Ahead

When I got engaged, the world took on a whole new light. I had worked really hard to convince this wonderful, beautiful woman that God had blessed me to know and love that I would make a good husband and that we would make a great couple together. Once accomplished, we set out to prepare for the wedding. There are many things that go into that planning and the two of us threw ourselves into it. Yet, when we went in to meet with the minister who would marry us, he made sure that we knew that we were not supposed to be planning just for the wedding, but for the marriage. If you follow God's lifelong plan, marriage is for a lifetime. There are many wonderful things to look forward to.

Salvation following God's plan is the same way. Salvation, like the wedding, is an event, yet like the marriage, is a journey that will last your whole life, but unlike the marriage, continues on forever. Once you have accepted Christ as your Savior your life should be changed from that moment on. A new relationship should be fostered with our Lord and Savior that will have an impact in this life and beyond. Live today, tomorrow and forever in a way that acknowledges heaven in the future, and heaven on earth.

- Taking the right path
    - The way is through The Son.

- Paying the price
  - o You can't "good" yourself to heaven.

- Watching God work
  - o Look around you and see what God is doing.

- Looking forward
  - o What will we be like?

- Go tell it on the mountain
  - o Salvation starts here and now.

Challenge:

Men: Discuss with your young man the deeper meaning of God's salvation. Help him realize the strength that comes from God today and the hope of heaven in the future.

Young Men: Understand that salvation is not just about going to heaven in the future, but is real to you today and has an impact on your life here on earth.

Salvation – Taking the Road Ahead

Monday

Verse: 1 John 5:11

And this is the testimony: God has given us eternal life, and this life is in his Son.

Father's Thoughts: Now that we have discussed the how and why of salvation. Take some time as man and youth to discuss the concept of eternal life.

Sons' Thoughts: We have only one choice for eternal life, and God provided that in the person of his son, Jesus Christ.

Discussion Questions: Having that promise, the promise of salvation through Christ Jesus, what should that mean in how you live life daily, in your relationships, in how you spend your time?

Notes: _____
_____
_____
_____

Tuesday

Verse: Hebrews 9:15

> *For this reason Christ is the mediator of the new covenant that those who are called may receive the promised eternal inheritance—now that he has died as a ransom to set them free from the sins committed under the first covenant.*

Father's Thoughts: God's original covenant given to draw man to him was through the laws he established. This gave man guidance and knowledge of what was expected of him by God. How a man put his heart into this covenant was how they would be judged, but the outcome was the same, all sinned. To fulfill that relationship with God took a true mediator, one that could bridge the gap between God and man. This came through Jesus Christ, God's son.

Sons' Thoughts: Christ is basically the middle man when it comes to our relationship with God. As a mediator, he brought us and God together.

Discussion Questions: Mediation is the act of bridging the relationship between two parties who cannot separately get together. Why do you think such a mediator was necessary?

Notes: _____
_____
_____
_____

Wednesday

Verse: Deuteronomy 4:35

You were shown these things so that you might know that the Lord is God; besides him there is no other.

Father's Thoughts: God will reveal himself to you as you seek him. When you look at the wonderful nature surrounding you, when you feel the stirring within your soul longing for something bigger than yourself, it is not just to amaze, amuse and entertain you, it is his call for you to accept him, to know him and to love him.

Sons' Thoughts: Miracles aren't something that you see every day, but if you look for God's hand in certain things, you will definitely notice how he is at work in your life.

Discussion Questions: Look around, look at the way you are wonderfully made, the talents God has given you. Are you ready to know him, to accept him to become the child of God forever?

Notes: _____
_____
_____
_____

Thursday

Verse: 1 John 3:2

> *Dear friends, now we are children of God, and what we will be has not yet been made known. But we know that when he appears, we shall be like him, for we shall see him as he is.*

Father's Thoughts: What does it mean to be like Christ? We can only imagine. Salvation has an end that is no end at all. Eternal life in Christ means being in the presence of God FOREVER. As we grow closer to Him in this present life we start to get a glimpse of what this means, the peace, the confidence, the trust in His strength.

Sons' Thoughts: We shall be like him. We strive every day to do just that, but fall way short. I can't wait to be like Christ, and that is what we should hope to be.

Discussion Questions: How can you begin to move towards being more like Christ? What things in your life are keeping you separated from Him? As you grow in your relationship, are you sharing this with others?

Notes: _____
_____
_____
_____

Friday

Verse: 2 Timothy 1:8-10

> *So do not be ashamed to testify about our Lord, or ashamed of me his prisoner. But join with me in suffering for the gospel, by the power of God, who has saved us and called us to a holy life—not because of anything we have done but because of his own purpose and grace. This grace was given us in Christ Jesus before the beginning of time, but it has now been revealed through the appearing of our Savior, Christ Jesus, who has destroyed death and has brought life and immortality to light through the gospel.*

Father's Thoughts: Isn't it great to have a plan? Sometimes it may be fun to wing it, to improvise, to ad lib, but when thing get complicated it is great to have a plan that you can fall back on. God's salvation of man was planned, thought out, from the beginning of time. God knew that we as man would fail, but he had a plan. That plan is salvation through grace given us in Jesus. Immortality, eternal life, closeness to God, what a plan.

Sons' Thoughts: We will suffer while trying to do God's will. God tells us that right here. Paul is extending an invitation to us to join him in trying to live a godly life.

Discussion Questions: Have you accepted His plan? Are there friends at school who need to hear from you about God's great plan?

Notes: _____
_____
_____
_____

Week 22

Taking a Stand – Steven's Example

I have the pleasure of knowing a number of people that I can't tell you much about. I know that sounds strange, but these people are currently serving in countries that don't know why they are there. Oh, they may be agriculture workers, teachers or business men, but they are, in reality, missionaries for Christ. The countries in which they serve are openly hostile to the Gospel of Jesus Christ so these men, women and children are running a great risk. Sometimes their views and actions are called into question by the local authorities and they are required to take a stand. They can be expelled, or as has happened before, they may be jailed or killed. Eric Liddell, the Scottish runner remembered in the movie "Chariots of Fire," returned to China after winning the Olympic gold medal. He was imprisoned by the Japanese during World War II and eventually died in captivity. Throughout his life Liddell took his stand for Christ no matter what the cost. It is said his last words were: "It's complete surrender."

- Taking your stand
    o Know what you are talking about.

- Taking the risk
    o Look them in the eye.

- Finding your voice
    o Tough words – tough stance

- Knowing where to look
    o Seeing the right thing

- Coming to a bitter end
    o Could you forgive them?

Challenge:

Men: Following Christ can be tough, challenging and sometimes dangerous. Talk with your Young Man about these issues and the qualities it takes to remain strong in the face of adversity.

Young Men: Determine for yourself the type of man you want to be when facing tough, challenging and dangerous situations for Christ's sake.

Taking a Stand – Steven's Example

Monday

Verse: Acts 6:8-9

> *Now Stephen, a man full of God's grace and power, did great wonders and miraculous signs among the people. These men began to argue with Stephen, but they could not stand up against his wisdom or the Spirit by whom he spoke.*

Father's Thoughts: Stephen did wonders and signs, but how? By being full of God's grace and power. Men could not counter his words about Christ, why? Because of the wisdom and the Holy Spirit which came through his relationship with Christ. When we are called to make a stand for our faith, if we rely on our own power or we are weak in our relationship with Christ, we will fail.

Sons' Thoughts: Knowledge about the scriptures is great, but you have to be able to apply it to real life such as Stephen did here.

Discussion Questions: What are things you can do to strengthen your relationship with God through Christ so that you can stand up to tests of your faith, so you can take a bold stand?

Notes: _____
_____
_____
_____

Tuesday

Verse: Acts 6:9-10, 12

> *Opposition arose, however, from members of the Synagogue of the Freedmen (as it was called)—Jews of Cyrene and Alexandria as well as the provinces of Cilicia and Asia. Then they secretly persuaded some men to say, "We have heard Stephen speak words of blasphemy against Moses and against God." So they stirred up the people and the elders and the teachers of the law. They seized Stephen and brought him before the Sanhedrin.*

Father's Thoughts: Taking a stand for God means taking risks. Teenagers especially can deal with some very cruel and real opposition it they are speaking up for Jesus. Stephen came against the full force of those who would do anything, even lie, to fight against the truth of our salvation.

Sons' Thoughts: People will always find some way to put you down, no matter what you say. They knew what Stephen was saying was the truth, but they didn't want to hear it, so they made up stuff in order to get him in trouble. This could happen to anyone and we must be ready to stand up for our beliefs and for God.

Discussion Questions: What kinds of opposition do Christians face at your school? Do you feel if you take a stand for Christ that you will be openly opposed?

Notes: _____
_____
_____
_____

Wednesday

Verse: Acts 6:51-53

> *"You stiff-necked people, with uncircumcised hearts and ears! You are just like your fathers: You always resist the Holy Spirit! Was there ever a prophet your fathers did not persecute? They even killed those who predicted the coming of the Righteous One. And now you have betrayed and murdered him—you who have received the law that was put into effect through angels but have not obeyed it."*

Father's Thoughts: You know, I am not sure that I would have had the guts to tell a group that looked like they were about to kill me that they were "stiff-necked". (By the way, what is 'stiff-necked'?) Yet Stephen stood his ground, told it like it was, even at the risk of his own life.

Sons' Thoughts: Here is Stephen standing up for himself. He told off this group of liars and hypocrites with some serious accusations. He told them what he thought and probably echoed what God thought about them.

Discussion Questions: Are we tough enough to take a firm stand? Are we willing to confront sin even if it means conflict?

Notes: _____
_____
_____
_____

Thursday

Verse: Acts 6:54-56

> *When they heard this, they were furious and gnashed their teeth at him. But Stephen, full of the Holy Spirit, looked up to heaven and saw the glory of God, and Jesus standing at the right hand of God. "Look," he said, "I see heaven open and the Son of Man standing at the right hand of God."*

Father's Thoughts: Again we see Stephen facing the angry mob. I don't know if you or I will ever come to this point or not. If we do, I hope and pray that we will be 'full of the Holy Spirit,' willing to take a stand and be witnesses for Him.

Sons' Thoughts: God readily accepts Stephen into heaven to join him. It brings God great pleasure when his people stand up for him, and show their zeal and love for him.

Discussion Questions: Are you willing to follow the Spirit's direction in the face of an angry world?

Notes: _____
_____
_____
_____

Friday

Verse: Acts 6:57-60

> *At this they covered their ears and, yelling at the top of their voices, they all rushed at him, dragged him out of the city and began to stone him. Meanwhile, the witnesses laid their clothes at the feet of a young man named Saul. While they were stoning him, Stephen prayed, "Lord Jesus, receive my spirit." Then he fell on his knees and cried out, "Lord, do not hold this sin against them." When he had said this, he fell asleep.*

Father's Thoughts: Persecution came to its worst end, death. More and more people are opposing the stand that Christians are taking these days. Will it come to violence? I don't know, but it could. You may be called to ministry in other parts of the world where there is violent persecution such as the Middle East and parts of Asia.

Sons' Thoughts: Even at his last word, Stephen is praying to God. He even asks that his persecutors be forgiven. Only someone with an immense love for God and others could have asked for something like that.

Discussion Questions: How then will you approach the risks involved? Will you be willing to take a stand like Stephen, will you be able to forgive like Stephen?

Notes: _____
_____
_____
_____

Week 23

Taking a Stand – Elijah's Example

Are Christians wimps? Let me see….Jesus and his brother James were carpenters. Well, there was very little wood in that part of the world so being a carpenter meant that you worked with wood and STONE. Jesus and his brothers were probably ripped. Then you take James and John, they were nicknamed Sons of Thunder. Simon, also a commercial fisherman, was renamed – The Rock. Okay, Matthew was a tax collector so maybe he was a bit soft but as far as the descriptions given to us in the Bible, the first Christians were a manly bunch of men. Paul even survived a stoning. Oh, did I mention the meek and mild John the Baptist? Bear Grylls has nothing on him.

Now take Elijah. He has the guts to stand up to 450 prophets of the idol Baal and challenge them to show that their god was real. Their god was usually made out of stone or wood in the shape of a bull to represent strength and fertility. Well, as you will read, Baal was a no-show and the true God, Jehovah, showed his power. This probably led to the phrase, No Bull.

- It's hard to balance on a fence.
    o Choose your side.

- The guilty dog barks the loudest.
    o Can it pass the test?

- Stand back and watch the BIG God.
  o Leave no doubt.

- What will survive the fire?
  o Proof in the poofing.

- Prove it.
  o And they will come.

Challenge:

Men: Teach your young man what a REAL man is like when faced with a challenge. Discuss what are the qualities that both of you have that would help you face all situations.

Young Men: Think about the tough situations that you might face while following Christ. Determine ahead of time how you might handle such situations and study the Word so that you will be prepared.

Taking a Stand – Elijah's Example

Monday

Verse: 1 Kings 18:21

> *Elijah went before the people and said, "How long will you waver between two opinions? If the LORD is God, follow him; but if Baal is God, follow him." But the people said nothing.*

Father's Thoughts: Lukewarm, wishy-washy, weak-spined. Not great ways to be described. How many weak people do you know that just will not make up their minds on what they believe? God wants real men, God wants strong men. If we say we are Christians, then we should act like it and take a stand.

Sons' Thoughts: Make up your mind. If you want to follow God, follow him to the fullest. If not, don't even proclaim it. It is better if you don't pretend to love God than if you do and live a different lifestyle.

Discussion Questions: Have you been challenged about your faith? Have you ever been asked what you really believe? How did you respond? How should you respond?

Notes: _____
_____
_____
_____

Tuesday

Verse: 1 Kings 18:25-29

> *Elijah said to the prophets of Baal, "Choose one of the bulls and prepare it first, since there are so many of you. Call on the name of your god, but do not light the fire." So they took the bull given them and prepared it. Then they called on the name of Baal from morning till noon. "O Baal, answer us!" they shouted. But there was no response; no one answered. And they danced around the altar they had made. And it came to pass at noon, that Elijah mocked them, and said, Cry aloud: for he is a god; either he is talking, or he is pursuing, or he is in a journey, or peradventure he sleepeth, and must be awaked. And they cried aloud, and cut themselves after their manner with knives and lancets, till the blood gushed out upon them. And it came to pass, when midday was past, and they prophesied until the time of the offering of the evening sacrifice, that there was neither voice, nor any to answer, nor any that regarded.*

Father's Thoughts: Can a piece of gold or wood bring you power and happiness? Idols come in all shapes and sizes. It can be money, it can be fame, it can be popularity but none of these, or anything has any power. No matter how much you work at it, THEY CAN'T HEAR YOU, THEY CAN'T HELP YOU!

Sons' Thoughts: Elijah puts God and Baal to the test here. He wants to see the prophets of Baal answer to him and to God, but as predicted, Baal is a no-show.

Discussion Questions: What part of your life, or what things in your life are you putting before God? When you really need help, do these things pass the test?

Notes:

Wednesday

Verse: 1 Kings 18:32-33

With the stones he built an altar in the name of the LORD, and he dug a trench around it large enough to hold two seahs of seed. He arranged the wood, cut the bull into pieces and laid it on the wood. Then he said to them, "Fill four large jars with water and pour it on the offering and on the wood."

Father's Thoughts: What kind of "guts" do you have when facing questions about your faith in Jesus Christ? We can be confident that no matter what the circumstances our God can overcome any obstacle that can be put in our way.

Sons' Thoughts: He really trusts God here to be able to take a set-up like this and risks his reputation as a man of God. If God doesn't come through here, he would most likely be killed.

Discussion Questions: Do you really have full confidence in God and the salvation he gives through Christ? Are you willing to have it put to the test? How might it be tested in your daily life?

Notes: _____
_____
_____
_____

Thursday

Verse: 1 Kings 18:37-38

> *Answer me, O LORD, answer me, so these people will know that you, O LORD, are God, and that you are turning their hearts back again." Then the fire of the LORD fell and burned up the sacrifice, the wood, the stones and the soil, and also licked up the water in the trench.*

Father's Thoughts: The power of being connected to God is evident. Someone does not just jump up one day and say, "God, do this, or God, do that." Elijah had a deep relationship with God and, then, his prayers were answered.

Sons' Thoughts: Of course God comes through for Elijah in this difficult test. The prophets of Baal are left empty-handed as nothing happens to their altar. God, though, reins down fire and proves his existence to the people of Baal.

Discussion Questions: What are you doing on a daily basis to make sure you are connected to God?

Notes: _____
_____
_____
_____

Friday

Verse: 1 Kings 18:39

And when all the people saw it, they fell on their faces: and they said, The LORD, he is the God; the LORD, he is the God.

Father's Thoughts: What an impact we can have when we stand up for God! The evidence is clear by what God showed through this man who dared to take a risk and stand against the forces of evil. I can only hope that more Christian men, young and old, will take up the cause of good and confront evil at every turn.

Sons' Thoughts: You know Elijah must've been feeling pretty darn good right about then. He had just shown all of Baal's followers just how powerful his God was. But we must be careful of these times where God works through us. Now realize the subject in that sentence was God. He is the one who works through us, and we must be careful to step down off of our loftiest throne and give Him the deserved glory.

Discussion Questions: Who is the boldest Christian that you know? How have they used that boldness to witness for Christ? What can you do make that a characteristic of your life?

Notes: _____
_____
_____
_____

Week 24

Taking a Stand – Unlikely Heroes

—⚬—

Under what circumstances are you going to take the biggest risk? If you have to face down an enemy and fight, what will be your motivation? "No greater love has a man than that he would lay it down for his friends." These are Jesus' words as He was beginning to reveal to His disciples that he would die on the cross. In the multitude of wars that have been fought, of the battles that have raged, the love of friends and family are a motivating and driving force to fight for what is right and what is good. As Christian men, we are to be the standard bearers in standing up for our family, for our friends, and for our Christian brothers and sisters. It may mean that you have to take risks and you may suffer for it.

Sometimes the stand you take may be against your friends. That may happen when your friends or family are asking you to discard your integrity, your principles and to deny God. These may be some of the greatest battles that you face because of the love and respect you have for the very ones who are telling you to do the wrong thing. This is when you will be called to be a man, and from Job and Esther (that's right, a woman), you can learn these lessons well.

- Risking it all
  - Family first

- Open your eyes
  - See the risk and have the passion to do something.

- Turn the tables
  - Let God do His work.

- He's coming after you
  - Be on your guard.

- They may be related
  - But can still be wrong

Challenge:

Men: Discuss the bonds of family and friends when facing tough and challenging situations. Give your Young Man examples from your own life of how you have had to stand up for your family, and sometimes against your friends.

Young Men: Discuss how friendships and family relationships shape your life. Resolve to keep things in perspective when facing difficult times and trust God to lead you through.

Taking a Stand – Unlikely Heroes

Monday

Verse: Esther 8:3

Esther again pleaded with the king, falling at his feet and weeping. She begged him to put an end to the evil plan of Haman the Agagite, which he had devised against the Jews.

Father's Thoughts: In the right place, at the right time in history, that is the story of Esther. That however is not the end of the story. It is not just important to be in the right place, you have to take the right actions. You have to be willing to put yourself on the line in love.

Sons' Thoughts: Esther is an extremely strong woman. In a time where women were regarded more as property than as humans, she stands up to her husband, pleading for mercy for her people. We need to be willing to really stand up for something that we believe in, no matter what our status.

Discussion Questions: Where has God put you? What injustices do you see and are you gutsy enough to stand up for what is right, even at a risk?

Notes: _____
_____
_____
_____

Tuesday

Verse: Esther 8:6

> *For how can I bear to see disaster fall on my people? How can I bear to see the destruction of my family?"*

Father's Thoughts: One of the hardest things to do in life is to look outside yourself and focus on others' needs, wants, cares and safety. Esther shows the type of courage that most men cannot muster. Bravery knows no sex or age, no economic or social standing.

Sons' Thoughts: Esther truly mourns for her people. She does not want to see them killed or destroyed, and knows that she must do something to preserve their well- being.

Discussion Questions: Who do you know that has really shown unselfish bravery? What characteristic of this person stands out to you that you would like to emulate?

Notes: _____
_____
_____
_____

Wednesday

Verse: Esther 9:1

> *On the thirteenth day of the twelfth month, the month of Adar, the edict commanded by the king was to be carried out. On this day the enemies of the Jews had hoped to overpower them, but now the tables were turned and the Jews got the upper hand over those who hated them.*

Father's Thoughts: Because of Esther's bravery God honored her actions and saved her people. Risking it all, she put herself on the line and the enemies had the tables turned on them. We have a common enemy, Satan, and he wants to destroy our people and our families. What a wonderful thought that our bravery might turn the tables on Satan and save our family from destruction.

Sons' Thoughts: God will come through for you when you are down. Sometimes you think that you are at the absolute worst point, but then everything shifts in the exact opposite direction, and starts going the right way.

Discussion Questions: What enemy does your family face? How can you be used as an instrument to turn the tide and fight off these enemies?

Notes: _____
_____
_____
_____

Thursday

Verse: Job 1:8

> *Then the LORD said to Satan, "Have you considered my servant Job? There is no one on earth like him; he is blameless and upright, a man who fears God and shuns evil."*

Father's Thoughts: Get ready, when God has good things to say about you, it really ticks Satan off. Satan will pretty much leave you alone when you are floundering, but when you fear God and shun evil; he will come at you with his very worst. Job had built a firm foundation with his trust and reverence of the Almighty. It was that trust, reverence and desire to please God that got him through the worst times. Job could stand the pressure because he had already stood for God.

Sons' Thoughts: Job must have been one really special guy to have the highest God bragging about him. God is perfect, so to have him saying these things about you must really mean something.

Discussion Questions: What can you do to build your foundation strong enough to withstand Satan's ire? How can the men of your family bond together to fight him off?

Notes: _____
_____
_____
_____

Friday

Verse: Job 2:9-10

> *His wife said to him, "Are you still holding on to your integrity? Curse God and die!" He replied, "You are talking like a foolish woman. Shall we accept good from God, and not trouble?" In all this, Job did not sin in what he said.*

Father's Thoughts: The bigger they are the harder they fall, or so the saying goes. In this case, and the same holds true today, Satan attacks those that he knows are living for God. There is nothing he wants more than to bring down the effective witness, the preacher who is winning souls, the missionary on the front lines, the young man saying no to the sins of this world and impacting his school. During those attacks people around you will question your trials, question your reasons for continuing to trust God.

Sons' Thoughts: Sometimes we have to look at priorities. When Job's wife tells him to curse God, he does not give in to temptation and please her by doing it, but he does what he knows is right and sticks to his godly tendencies.

Discussion Questions: Will you give in to the temptation to blame God or will you accept and grow in his true will? Which of your friends or family discourage you from doing what is right? How can you stand up to them like Job stood up to his wife?

Notes: _____
_____
_____
_____

Week 25

I Know It's Tempting but……..

—⚏—

The lyrics of a song go, "Hit 'em when they're up, hit em when they're down." In a nutshell you have one of Satan's philosophies of temptation. When you are way up there on top of the world, you've just hit the homerun, that girl you have wanted to go out with just said yes, the curtain closed and you realize they were giving you a standing ovation, Satan can strike. He can tempt you to take God for granted and take the glory for yourself. Satan can also hit you when you are down, when you made a big mistake, or you are just tired of life. He can tempt you to feel sorry for yourself, to blame others, to lash out at others. He can tempt you to ease the pain through some form of escape.

Satan even tried this with Jesus. He tried to get Jesus to break His fasting and prayer in a selfish and artificial manor. Satan tempted Jesus with power and riches that were outside the Father's plan for Him. Satan tempted Jesus to show off His powers of faith for His own glory. Throughout these temptations, Jesus showed men how they should stand up to them and proved that true manhood is being true to God.

- Coming down off the mountain
    - Hit 'em while their down.

- Chewing on a rock
  - Beware of what looks tasty.

- Way up high
  - Beware the promise.

- The big throw down
  - Beware the attention.

- The end of round one
  - There will be a next time.

Challenge:

Men: Walk your Young Man through the things in life that will tempt a man. Give him the tools that he will need to fight off Satan's best shots.

Young Men: Look at the things that tempt you the most and develop a game plan for how you will fight them off.

I Know It's Tempting but……..

Monday

Verse: Luke 4:1-2

> *Jesus, full of the Holy Spirit, returned from the Jordan and was led by the Spirit in the desert, where for forty days he was tempted by the devil. He ate nothing during those days and at the end of them he was hungry.*

Father's Thoughts: Jesus knew temptation was coming. He was at the high point of his ministry and he knew that the next step would be to die on the cross. He did not enter the desert to be tempted alone. He was "full of the Holy Spirit". He had prepared himself well for the onslaught. As a young man focused on doing the will of God, Satan will come after you. You must be prepared mentally, physically and spiritually. Spiritually is the most important because when you are down mentally and physically, Satan will strike.

Sons' Thoughts: Forty days seems a very long time to be doing absolutely nothing but be tempted. Think about it, there is absolutely nothing to do, you can't eat, and you can't take your mind off of anything but what the devil wants you to do. He was probably very weak from lack of sustenance, but he still held strong and resisted temptation.

Discussion Questions: How have you prepared yourself for the challenges ahead?

Notes: _____
_____
_____
_____

Tuesday

Verse: Luke 4:3-4

> *The devil said to him, "If you are the Son of God, tell this stone to become bread." Jesus answered, "It is written: 'Man does not live on bread alone"*

Father's Thoughts: We are so tied to our physical needs. Sometimes we can put our needs and desires before God's will. Jesus understood this and when He faced temptation he recognized that while God wants to give us our basic bodily needs, he also has much more for us. He recognized that God wants to fulfill us totally and that we should not depend on substitutes that offer only a part of His ideal for us.

Sons' Thoughts: Satan, as usual, hits us where we are the weakest. I can't go more than a few hours without food, and Jesus has been out there for forty days. Jesus knows the way Satan works, and hits him back where Satan can't respond, with scripture.

Discussion Questions: Are you willing to take the totality of what God has to offer you versus the quick easy way of partial satisfaction?

Notes: _____
_____
_____
_____

Wednesday

Verse: Luke 4:5-8

> *The devil led him up to a high place and showed him in an instant all the kingdoms of the world. And he said to him "I will give you all the authority and splendor, for it has been given to me, and I can give it to anyone I want to. So if you worship me, it will be all yours." Jesus answered, "It is written: 'Worship the Lord God and serve Him only.'*

Father's Thoughts: Power! We all want it, are tempted by it. There is an old phrase... power corrupts, absolute power corrupts absolutely. As men, we love power, power over our own bodies, power over situations, power over others. Satan wanted Christ to give up His relationship with God. Ultimately, that is what Satan wants us all to give up. Jesus knows the answer. His relationship with God was more important than all the power in the world. Can you fight the temptation of power?

Sons' Thoughts: Satan had no authority to give Jesus what he said he would, but Jesus, who is knowledgeable of all things, knows that the Lord God has the authority and allows Satan to do what he does.

Discussion Questions: What are you willing to give up to have power? Your integrity? Your sense of justice? Can you fight the temptation of power?

Notes: _____
_____
_____
_____

Thursday

Verse: Luke 4:9-12

> *The devil led him to Jerusalem and had him stand on the highest point of the temple. "If you are the Son of God," he said, "throw yourself down from here. For it is written: "'He will command his angels concerning you to guard you carefully; they will lift you up in their hands, so that you will not strike your foot against a stone.'" Jesus answered, "It says:, 'Do not put the Lord God to the test.' "*

Father's Thoughts: Young men are often guilty of drawing attention to themselves. That's the temptation that Jesus faced. "Hey, look at me, I can do anything. I am 10 feet tall and bulletproof." Yes, God loves us and wants to protect us. Yet, he wants us to focus on Him, not have us constantly trying and testing His love and patience. Satan knew this temptation, Christ knew this temptation.

Sons' Thoughts: Satan is hoping that Jesus will get sick of him and prove once and for all that he is the Christ, therefore bowing to his wishes. Jesus again outsmarts him by quoting scripture.

Discussion Questions: Can you as a young man recognize this temptation and like Jesus, have the Word in your heart not to fall to it?

Notes: _____
_____
_____
_____

Friday

Verse: Luke 4:13

> *When the devil had finished all this tempting, he left him until an opportune time.*

Father's Thoughts: You have successfully resisted temptation. You said no when you needed to, said yes when you needed to, trusted God with the situation, and the worst is over, right? Not quite. Your walk with the Lord will be a lifelong journey, you will need to continue with your Bible study and prayer so that the next time, and there will be a next time, that Satan finds opportunity, he will be back. It may be tomorrow, but could be in the next five minutes.

Sons' Thoughts: Satan is very smart, and only hits us when he knows we will be vulnerable. He wouldn't tempt us to cuss in church because he knows that we are smarter than that. He will wait until we are in a situation where peer pressure and other factors cause us to stumble more easily.

Discussion Questions: Knowing he will be back to tempt you again, what steps can you take in your life to be prepared?

Notes: _____
_____
_____
_____

Week 26

Faith – Go Sit in That Chair

Look over there, a chair sits in the corner waiting for you. It is a comfortable chair with a table next to it. The lighting is good and a great book awaits you. You think that chair will hold your weight; you believe that is it well built, strong, and fit for its purpose. Your family bought that chair specifically to have a great spot to read, to rest and relax. That is belief. It is easy to believe something, to know something deep down in your heart, but are you willing to put faith to it?

The real difference between knowing something and having faith in it is the willingness to take action, to put it to the test. When you approach that chair, turn around and sit on it, then belief turns into faith. It is the same with Jesus. We can believe in the person and purpose of Jesus as savior, but we must be willing to put Him to the test, to take the action on that belief and turn it into faith.

- Are you sure?
    - o Do you have to see to believe?

- Going for hope
    - o Are you strong enough to wait?

- Excuse me, please move that mountain
    - o Won't take much

- Nobody knows the trouble I've seen
  - Trust me.

- It takes two
  - Mix 'em up.

Challenge:
Men: Encourage your Young Man to learn to trust in God and have faith in him at all times. Help them learn that faith is a verb and that faith is a call to action.
Young Men: Look at areas in your life where you need to put faith in God. Find ways that you can put that faith into action.

Faith – Go Sit in That Chair

Monday

Verse: Hebrews 11:1

> *Now faith is being sure of what we hope for and certain of what we do not see.*

Father's Thoughts: Faith is a verb, it is active, it's putting your beliefs into action and dealing with certainty, being sure, and doing it. It takes a man-sized level of strength and character to take action on something we cannot see.

Sons' Thoughts: The physical world is very concrete. Believing something outside of it is very hard for us to do, as visual, sensual beings.

Discussion Questions: Where in your life do you need to move from belief to faith?

Notes: _____
_____
_____
_____

Tuesday

Verse: Romans 4:12

Against all hope, Abraham in hope believed and so became the father of many nations, just as it had been said to him, "So shall your offspring be."

Father's Thoughts: "You're hopeless!" I hope that I have never said those words to you. I wish no parent would ever utter those words. I guess that Abraham must have felt like that word described him. But in spite of that, he put his hope in one place, God. He did not put it in other men; they can let you down. He did not put it in religion or even in himself; he put his hope, his faith, in Almighty God and was rewarded. Abraham set the ultimate example of faith.

Sons' Thoughts: Abraham was just one man. I know it would be crazy to suggest that one person could be the start of something like an entire nation of people. "Against all hope" is something that is very common to say. To us, it may seem impossible, but impossibility is something that does not apply to God.

Discussion Questions: When you are struggling and feel that hope is lost, can you take his example and put your faith in the one true God?

Notes: _____
_____
_____
_____

Wednesday

Verse: Matthew 17:20

> *He replied, "Because you have so little faith. I tell you the truth, if you have faith as small as a mustard seed, you can say to this mountain, 'Move from here to there' and it will move. Nothing will be impossible for you."*

Father's Thoughts: Sometimes it is easy to feel inadequate, especially if we have examples of giants around us. There will always be someone bigger, stronger, with more faith, more trust and it can be intimidating. Jesus said that we do not have to be "Faith Giants" to get his attention. That is the good thing about faith, we just have to have it, even just a little bit and God can work with it. It is not the size of the faith; it is the sincerity of it and in whom you put that faith.

Sons' Thoughts: Our faith is the basis for our abilities. With running, if you don't believe that you can run a certain time or beat a certain person, chances are that you won't. You have to have confidence in God and yourself that you can do things that you never dreamed possible.

Discussion Questions: Are you ready to put that faith in the one that can move mountains with you as the tool?

Notes: _____
_____
_____
_____

Thursday

Verse: John 14:1

> *"Do not let your hearts be troubled. Trust in God, trust also in me."*

Father's Thoughts: In the worst of times, whom do you trust? When everything seems to be stacked against you, whom do you trust? Jesus was talking to His disciples a couple of days before he was to be crucified. He knew this would be the toughest of times for them. For several years they had invested their lives in following Him and now he was going to die. His words were simple, "trust me". We have to have faith in the toughest of times and that faith comes from taking God at His word and trusting Him. Trust him that through Christ, He has our back.

Sons' Thoughts: When times get tough, it is essential to look to God for guidance.

Discussion Questions: Can you learn to trust him in your toughest hours?

Notes: _____
_____
_____
_____

Friday

Verse: James 2:14

> *What good is it, my brothers, if a man claims to have faith but has no deeds, can such a faith save him?*

Father's Thoughts: We talked about faith being action, it also has legs. Faith is something that needs to be shared with others. Shared with your classmates, and shared with the kids in your neighborhood.

Sons' Thoughts: Faith should follow from the inside to the outside. If outward deeds are the only thing that happens, your faith is not real. If it is truly an inward change of heart, it should lead to outward actions automatically.

Discussion Questions: Together, list 3 to 5 things that you can do now to put your faith into actions. Make them practical things that you can do together.

Notes: _____
_____
_____
_____

Week 27

What Do You Want To Be When You Grow Up - I

What does it really mean to be a Godly man? If you think about it too long your head may spin and you may become overwhelmed with all the things you think you might have to be or do. Before you get too wrapped up and feel inadequate, it might be good to just list some characteristics that a Christian man ought to display and see examples of this behavior. Then think of the Christian men that you know and admire.

So when you look in the mirror, when you search your heart and take stock in your attitude and actions, what do you see? When we are called to be followers of Christ, when we accept His salvation and allow the Holy Spirit to control us, we should see certain characteristic come to the top which define us as Christian men. Think about how you display some of the following.

- Strength and Courage
- Bravery
- Purity
- In control
- Differentiation

Challenge:

Men: Teach your Young Man the characteristics that God expects of all men. Give him practical examples from your own life and those of the men in your family.

Young Men: Define ways that you can exhibit these characteristics. What men do you know are examples of each one?

What Do You Want To Be When You Grow Up - I

Monday

Verse: Joshua 1:6-9

> "Be strong and courageous, because you will lead these people to inherit the land I swore to their forefathers to give them. Be strong and very courageous. Be careful to obey all the law my servant Moses gave you; do not turn from it to the right or to the left, that you may be successful wherever you go. Do not let this Book of the Law depart from your mouth; meditate on it day and night, so that you may be careful to do everything written in it. Then you will be prosperous and successful. Have I not commanded you? Be strong and courageous. Do not be terrified; do not be discouraged, for the LORD your God will be with you wherever you go."

Father's Thoughts: God so very much wants men who will be leaders. That does not mean every man will lead a great empire, not every man will be class president, company president or even a shift supervisor. Being a leader means stepping up to the plate when asked, regardless the size of the task. Leading is not something to be taken lightly. Why else would God have told Joshua three times "be strong and courageous." In this modern world we need strong and courageous high school club leaders, team leaders, discussion group leaders. We need strong and courageous fathers, coaches and teachers.

Sons' Thoughts: "Do not be timid" is the central theme here. If we cannot be strong in our faith, then it is obviously not that important to us. Our convictions should spill into every aspect of our lives.

Discussion Questions: What do you think gives us the strength and the courage to be Christian leaders in all circumstances?

Notes:

Tuesday

Verse: Numbers 14:6-9

> *Joshua son of Nun and Caleb son of Jephunneh, who were among those who had explored the land, tore their clothes and said to the entire Israelite assembly, "The land we passed through and explored is exceedingly good. If the LORD is pleased with us, he will lead us into that land, a land flowing with milk and honey, and will give it to us. Only do not rebel against the LORD. And do not be afraid of the people of the land, because we will swallow them up. Their protection is gone, but the LORD is with us. Do not be afraid of them."*

Father's Thoughts: What does it mean to be brave, to be fearless? As a man of God we should take on Joshua and Caleb's characteristics. They weren't crazy, they were not thrill seekers, they were simply young men that saw God's will and recognized who the strong one really is—God.

Sons' Thoughts: Why should we be afraid of any person or group of people? What are they going to do to us? Make fun of us? Hurt us? We shouldn't be worried about being judged by others.

Discussion Questions: When you come up against opposition to your faith—and you will—are you going to fret about how powerful the enemy appears, or are you going to recognize how much more powerful is your God?

Notes: _____
_____
_____
_____

Wednesday

Verse: Psalm 119:9-11

> *How can a young man keep his way pure? By living according to your word. I seek you with all my heart; do not let me stray from your commands. I have hidden your word in my heart that I might not sin against you.*

Father's Thoughts: When you think of manly characteristics, being lilly white pure may not be one of them. No, men like to get dirty, we like the smells of the outdoors, we like to feel free. The outside can get as dirty as you want, from a dirt standpoint, but to have the kind of relationship we need with God, our insides need to be spotless. We can't do that alone, we need the word of God. By keeping that cleansing agent inside we can fight off the infection of sin that could fester and cause us unimaginable pain.

Sons' Thoughts: The first thing you have to do if you want to stay pure is get into the Bible. Inevitably, when I was struggling with something, if I got into the Word and prayed about it, that temptation would become easier to deal with because I was letting God take care of the situation, and not trying to work it myself.

Discussion Questions: What are some of the steps you need to take in your daily life to make the word more meaningful to you?

Notes: _____
_____
_____
_____

Thursday

Verse: 2 Timothy 2:24-26

> *And the Lord's servant must not quarrel; instead, he must be kind to everyone, able to teach, not resentful. Those who oppose him he must gently instruct, in the hope that God will grant them repentance leading them to a knowledge of the truth, and that they will come to their senses and escape from the trap of the devil, who has taken them captive to do his will.*

Father's Thoughts: God wants His men to be gentle giants. We are called to be bold, strong, courageous, fearless and……..gentle. While at first that may seem to be counterintuitive it really makes sense. People respect strength, both physical and spiritual, but do not respond well to being intimidated either way. We have to look at the long term goal for those we are entrusted with as men and leaders, salvation and discipleship. We value strength, but value it with self-control.

Sons' Thoughts: We must be gentle in our dealings with people. If we want to be treated the same way that we treat others, we must put others' priorities first. If we do this, we will be given the satisfaction of knowing that others are seeing God's love through us.

Discussion Questions: Name a situation where controlled strength might work better than brute strength.

Notes: _____
_____
_____
_____

Friday

Verse: Joshua 3:5

> *Joshua told the people, "Consecrate yourselves, for tomorrow the LORD will do amazing things among you."*

Father's Thoughts: I love youth ministers. As a group they are usually the most enthusiastic ministers in the church. They use a lot of words like AWESOME, EXTREME, AMAZING and PUMPED UP. It is that kind of enthusiasm that I wish were infectious. I wish that as a Christian man I could be that kind of leader, teacher and father. Joshua must have been both enthusiastic and charismatic because through his leadership God did do AMAZING things.

Sons' Thoughts: Be ready. God is going to use you in ways that you never thought possible, and it could happen at any time.

Discussion Questions: What would it take to get you pumped up about doing the LORD's work?

Notes: _____
_____
_____

Week 28

What Do You Want To Be When You Grow Up - II

In some ways it is easy for young men to relate to the "hard" characteristics of a Christian man. As you discussed last week, a Christian man should be brave, courageous and strong. The strong man who truly seeks to follow our Lord Jesus Christ should strive for those characteristics that may seem "soft." The first deacons were not administrative leaders or enforcers, they were servers. Their kindness and love for the widows that they served was the catalyst for peace in the early church.

Men need to strive for characteristics that help them become constant ministers to the world where they live, work, or attend school. The characteristics discussed this week will help you become a better son, a better father, a creative and effective leader and employee. These "soft" attributes will make you a wonderful boyfriend and eventual husband. They will also serve to create the kind of friendships that will be unsinkable when the tough times of life inevitably hit.

- Wisdom
- Confidence
- Kindness
- Love
- Faithfulness

Challenge:

Men: Teach your Young Man the characteristics that God expects of all men. Give him practical examples from your own life and those of the men in your family.

Young Men: Define ways that you can exhibit these characteristics. What men do you know are examples of each one?

What Do You Want To Be When You Grow Up - II

Monday

Verse: Proverbs 4:5

> *Get wisdom, get understanding; do not forget my words or swerve from them.*

Father's Thoughts: One of the greatest gifts we can give to young men is the gift of ourselves. Being a mentor is both useful and rewarding as we can constantly be challenged to think. The goal of mentoring is not to do something for the one mentored, but to point the way, to encourage seeking. If each of us will endeavor to mentor those who come after us, we can point the way to wisdom, to understanding, and to the Word of God.

Sons' Thoughts: Solomon kind of flips what he means here. You need understanding, and you need wisdom, but where do you get those things? From the word of God. If you incorporate scripture into your life, you will become smarter and wiser.

Discussion Questions: To whom do you look for advice? Is it someone that you can respect, someone who is spiritually strong and mature? How can you accept mentoring and then pass that on by mentoring someone else?

Notes: _____
_____
_____

Tuesday

Verse: 1 John 3:21

> *Dear friends, if our hearts do not condemn us, we have confidence before God and receive from him anything we ask, because we obey his commands and do what pleases him.*

Father's Thoughts: Cause and effect. It is a concept that you have learned or will learn in high school. You push something, it will move. You put two certain chemicals together, you will get a reaction. If confidence to receive blessings before God is the desired effect, what is the cause? Obeying His commands and doing His will.

Sons' Thoughts: This is a little tricky. He says that if we have no sin, and we do exactly what God says, He will give us anything we want. We know that this is not possible, but if we strive to become this way, we have done what God asks us to.

Discussion Questions: What actions or activities in your life might be preventing you from receiving the full blessings God has to offer you?

Notes: _____
_____
_____
_____

Wednesday

Verse: 1 Thessalonians 5:15

Make sure that nobody pays back wrong for wrong, but always try to be kind to each other and to everyone else.

Father's Thoughts: Just like we talked about gentleness before, real men need to be fair, they need to be kind. How we handle relationships will be studied by those around us. As you enter manhood, you will increasingly see and experience conflict. We are told by the world that revenge is sweet. Sorry, there are many hurt and killed gang members that now know better. There can be a cycle of hurt/revenge/hurt again/revenge again that can go on and on, sometimes between men, families, even church groups. God's calling for us as men is to stand in that gap, to stop that cycle and restore justice, fairness, kindness. What situations have you seen or experienced at church, school, or home where you need to stop a harmful cycle?

Sons' Thoughts: All of us have been there before. We can't believe that he did that to us, and it is going to be awesome getting him back in an even more awful way than he can take. It is hard for our prideful self to be wronged and not retaliate. We don't want to appear weak, but God says that it takes even more strength to forgive that person for what he has done to us.

Discussion Questions: What situations have you seen or experienced at church, school or home where you need to stop a harmful cycle?

Notes: _____
_____
_____
_____

Thursday

Verse: 1 Corinthians 13:3

If I give all I possess to the poor and surrender my body to the flames, but have not love, I gain nothing.

Father's Thoughts: God wants his men to show generosity through love, never without it. That may not be the easiest thing in the world to accomplish. You may not really like the people with whom you need to be generous. You may not like everything that the church is doing and it may be tempting to tie generosity to 100% agreement. Instead, we should focus on loving those in need and giving because of that love.

Sons' Thoughts: It can be easy to do. We have service projects, Sunday School workdays, and chores to do. We can do them grudgingly or we can do them with enthusiasm and love. God wants us to do the latter, so as to let inward faith spill out in to the world.

Discussion Questions: What are some ways that you can focus on loving those that may not be likable?

Notes: _____
_____
_____
_____

Friday

Verse: Galatians 5:6

> *For in Christ Jesus neither circumcision nor uncircumcision has any value. The only thing that counts is faith expressing itself through love.*

Father's Thoughts: It's what's on the inside that counts, right? Everywhere we look we are bombarded by things geared towards enhancing our outward beauty. I am so sick of weight loss ads I could throw up. Well, maybe that would actually help me lose weight! Even in the church, as early as in the first church, there were people who would demand you had to do certain things, look certain ways, before you could be considered a Christian. It really only matters if the inside is right with God.

Sons' Thoughts: Petty religious acts do not please God. He wants a faith that is genuine, not worldly acts or signs that please other men. He does not want us to raise our hands in church only to show others how good we are, but to do everything for his glory.

Discussion Questions: Do we mix up our priorities trying to "look churchy'?

Notes: _____
_____
_____
_____

Week 29

Hang in There - I

If you don't like things right now, stick around. The only consistent thing about life is the constant change that is just around the corner. When I was ten years old, I thought life was pretty good. I lived in a "Leave it to Beaver" style suburb and life was simple and easy. Then my dad came in one day and announced that we were moving. Not only moving, but we were moving to Japan. I remember being filled with both anxiety and anticipation. My fifth grade teacher helped with the transition by throwing a big going-away party at a Japanese restaurant. The move went incredibly smooth and life in Japan was full of wonderful new experiences and freedoms that I never would have experienced back home. Then less than a year later we moved again, this time to Taiwan. This too was a great move, but two years later things changed dramatically. The U.S. began expanding relationships with China and the UN replaced Taiwan with the People's Republic of China.

Americans became targets of roving gangs who would throw rocks and bottles at us. One of my schoolmates was seriously injured when a large shard of glass hit him in the stomach. We were being persecuted just because we were Americans. We eventually moved on to Singapore but I will never forget the feeling of persecution. It gave me a brief glimpse of what the early Christians must have felt when they were persecuted, not for being from a different country but for following The Way. Together my friends and I were able to get past our rough spot but there are Christians all over the world that are being persecuted because of who they are and the Savior we serve. You may be having similar issues at school or work if you are bold about your faith.

- On trial
    - With a smile

- Standing up to the wind
    - Will get you noticed?

- What a character
    - Hope so

- Keep your eyes open
    - You know what's coming!

- Looking to the future
    - On my side

Challenge:
Men: Discuss the meaning of persecution. Talk about the ways that Christians face trials both at home and around the world and how we should view and react to them.

Young Men: Look at the things that you struggle with day to day. Begin to see how God supports you through the tough times.

Hang in There - I

Monday

Verse: James 1:2-3

Consider it pure joy, my brothers, whenever you face trials of many kinds, because you know that the testing of your faith develops perseverance.

Father's Thoughts: Sometimes I really hate these verses. I know I shouldn't, but I really have a hard time finding joy in my trials. But then I realize that the opposite of perseverance is giving up. I don't want to be a quitter; I really want to be known as someone who defies the odds and keeps going, and comes out on the other end better than when I started.

Sons' Thoughts: It is going to be tough to be a growing Christian. God tells us that flat out. If we expected this life to be easy, we were way off. Trials are going to come and how you deal with them shows God what kind of a person you really are.

Discussion Questions: What is an example of a time you had to persevere, to say no to quitting and to find joy in the problem you faced?

Notes: _____
_____
_____
_____

Tuesday

Verse: James 1:12

> *Blessed be the man who perseveres under trial, because when he has stood the test, he will receive the crown of life that God has promised to those who love him.*

Father's Thoughts: We have all heard the phrase, "what doesn't kill you makes you stronger." God understands that trials suffered for being His servant will be tough, but will be both a learning point here on earth as well as rewarded in heaven. Think about that when you think things are tough. Trust in this promise and keep going.

Sons' Thoughts: God loves to see us succeed. He wants to see us go up against the devil and show him that we are Men of God. If we can do this, our faith will grow and our relationship with God will prosper.

Discussion Questions: What trials are you facing in life, at work at school? Think of trials you have overcome, great or small. Did you learn something with the experience?

Notes: _____
_____
_____
_____

Wednesday

Verse: Romans 5:3-4

Not only so, but we also rejoice in our sufferings, because we know that suffering produces perseverance; perseverance, character; and character, hope.

Father's Thoughts: So here it is again, rejoice in our sufferings. Yesterday we talked about not being a quitter, but what does that lead to? Paul saw a progression: not quitting helps you to develop character and when you have character the people around you cannot help but notice the difference. That difference can give you confidence — hope —and your positive, hope -filled attitude can change lives.

Sons' Thoughts: Suffering is something that I have to deal with daily because of running, but I endure it because I know that through that suffering, I will become a better runner. So in the same way that physical suffering helps our physical body, emotional and spiritual suffering leads to a stronger emotional and spiritual person.

Discussion Questions: Are you so full of hope that it spills over and affects the people around you?

Notes: _____
_____
_____
_____

Thursday

Verse: 1 Thessalonians 3:3

We sent Timothy, who is our brother and God's fellow worker in spreading the gospel of Christ, to strengthen and encourage you in your faith, so that no one would be unsettled by these trials. You know quite well that we were destined for them. In fact, when we were with you, we kept telling you that we would be persecuted. And it turned out that way, as you well know.

Father's Thoughts: Trials are never meant to be endured alone. We all need strength and encouragement from our brothers in Christ. But don't be naïve, it also requires preparation. That is why there are several things you need to do to get ready for the persecution that will come: strengthen your fellowship with your Christian brothers, encourage each other daily in your faith, prepare yourself through prayer and study.

Sons' Thoughts: When someone comes to help you along with your faith, it is a good thing. Sometimes we feel that we don't need any help and that we can do it alone, but as brothers in Christ we should be able to share what we feel and think with others.

Discussion Questions: Who are two or three 'encouragers' with whom you can bond to prepare yourselves for the rough times?

Notes: _____
_____
_____
_____

Friday

Verse: Jeremiah 29:11

> *"For I know the plans I have for you," declares the LORD, "plans to prosper you and not to harm you, plans to give you hope and a future."*

Father's Thoughts: We may enjoy being random; it is fun to ad lib and to stretch ourselves, to learn to be flexible. However, when tough times hit, when things don't seem to be going well, all that randomness can suddenly feel like chaos. It's at these times when it is great to know someone has a plan. Better yet, that plan is from God and is uniquely developed for each of us.

Sons' Thoughts: When something bad happens, we are quick to find someone to blame, and sometimes that can be God, but He wants us to know that he wants us to prosper, and use everything in our life for the overall plan that he has set out for us.

Discussion Questions: How can God's plan bring you hope during the toughest times of your life?

Notes: _____
_____
_____
_____

Week 30

Hang in There - II

Two summers ago I had a chance to spend some time with missionaries that are in some of the most difficult areas on earth for Christians. In these unnamed countries the price that Christians pay for their faith can be severe. They can lose their homes, jobs, families and their lives for taking a public stand for Christ. Fortunately for us, God knew what we would be facing and gave us several gifts to overcome the persecution of this world. Among these are relationship, confidence and hope. We have both our relationship with God and with other Christians to give us strength. We have confidence that God will be with us in all trials. We also have the hope that our God has all things both now and forever in His hands.

With these gifts and others we can move forward to take risks and boldly proclaim His kingdom. You may not be called to go into the jungles of a hostile country. You will be called to go into the jungles of the world around you. You will not always be welcomed, you may even be viciously attacked, but the gifts of God will allow you to keep your head held high and Christian brothers will be there to support you.

- What's in a name
    o What are you called?

- Never more than you can bear
  - A way out

- This, too, shall pass
  - It's all temporary

- A really big stick
  - Nice weapon

- Give me your best shot
  - Still not bad enough

Challenge:
Men: Discuss the meaning of persecution. Talk about the ways that Christians face trials both at home and around the world and how we should view and react to them.
Young Men: Look at the things that you struggle with day to day. Begin to see how God supports you through the tough times.

Hang in There - II

Monday

Verse: Genesis 32:28

> *Then the man said, "Your name will no longer be Jacob, but Israel, [which means he struggles with God] because you have struggled with God and with men and have overcome."*

Father's Thoughts: What is in a name? God changed several people's names, think of Saul (Paul), Simon (Peter), and Abram (Abraham). These men needed a new start, a fresh perspective and a new identity – IN GOD. We may not change our name, but we all need to look to God for renewal through His son Jesus Christ.

Sons' Thoughts: While it seems strange to us that God would give someone a new name just for overcoming some obstacle in his life, Jacob needed a reminder of why he was there and of his struggles in life. This reminder would make him always look back on what had happened earlier in his life.

Discussion Questions: Are there times that you would like to change your identity? Have you surrendered your life to Christ so that He can renew you to His purpose?

Notes: _____
_____
_____
_____

Tuesday

Verse: 1 Corinthians 10:13

No temptation has seized you except what is common to man. And God is faithful; he will not let you be tempted beyond what you can bear. But when you are tempted, he will also provide a way out so that you can stand up under it.

Father's Thoughts: Isn't it nice to know you are not alone? No matter what problem or trial you face, someone has gone through it before. Even better, we have a Savior who came to earth as a man and was tempted and tried just like us. God will hold his end of the bargain and will show you the way out of a situation whether it is initial temptation or a long trial.

Sons' Thoughts: There is no temptation that we cannot deal with along with God's help. I know that there are some very tempting things out there, and that there seems to be no way that we can overcome them, but if we just ask God to help us, we can get through anything.

Discussion Questions: How can fellowship with other Christians help in this process?

Notes: _____
_____
_____
_____

Wednesday

Verse: 2 Corinthians 4:17

For our light and momentary troubles are achieving for us an eternal glory that far outweighs them all.

Father's Thoughts: How do we react when things are going wrong? In the moment it can seem like the biggest, baddest issue in the world. Just like some people are afraid of shots, they squirm and fidget and get all worked up over what will last say, 2.352 seconds, maybe the after effect will last another hour or two and then only in the 1 - 2 inches around where we got the shot. In the scheme of things that is such a small thing to get worked up about. Paul indicates that our trials are like a shot, light and momentary, and in perspective to the wonderful life, the eternal life that God gives us through Jesus, is so much bigger and greater that these pains.

Sons' Thoughts: When a race or a match begins to get hard, the pain can really begin to creep in, first slowly and then an all-out assault. Why would someone put themselves through that? Because of the reward at the end. Anything that we have to go through is outweighed by the feeling of a job well done, and the rewards always outweigh the pain.

Discussion Questions: Look back on some trouble or hard time you had in the past. Does it not seem small now in comparison to life as a whole?

Notes: _____
_____
_____
_____

Thursday

Verse: 2 Corinthians 10:4

> *The weapons we fight with are not the weapons of the world. On the contrary, they have divine power to demolish strongholds.*

Father's Thoughts: Think back to the armor of God. The shield, the helmet, the sword. When you have to deal with tough times you have such great gifts that you can wield. They are weapons of such enormous power that nothing can withstand them. But you have to use them; a sword in its sheath is useless. A helmet or shield on the shelf collects dust.

Sons' Thoughts: We may not think ourselves capable of handling things of this world that are battling against us, but God says that we have the means and weapons to conquer anything that we put our minds to.

Discussion Questions: What do you think the best offensive weapon is to use when you are facing tough issues?

Notes: _____
_____
_____
_____

Friday

Verse: Luke 9:23-27

> *And he said to them all, if any man will come after me, let him deny himself, and take up his cross daily, and follow me. For whosoever will save his life shall lose it: but whosoever will lose his life for my sake, the same shall save it. For what is a man advantaged, if he gain the whole world, and lose himself, or be cast away? For whosoever shall be ashamed of me and of my words, of him shall the Son of man be ashamed, when he shall come in his own glory, and in his Father's, and of the holy angels. But I tell you of a truth, there be some standing here, which shall not taste of death, till they see the kingdom of God.*

Father's Thoughts: Death holds both a mystery and fear for most, if not all people. Even more so for those who do not know Christ. We are called to follow Him daily, to make a full sacrifice for Him regardless of the circumstances or consequences. Once we plunge into this life of sacrifice we will see Him work in mighty ways. We who follow Christ do not have to wait for death to see His Kingdom here on earth. Death then holds no fear for us for we have a hope that only those who believe on Jesus can know.

Sons' Thoughts: This is why we live. Death is put forward as a terrible thing, and it certainly can be for those who are left here on earth without a loved one, but death will seem like nothing when we enter into eternity.

Discussion Questions: Discuss death and dying. Are you afraid? How can you work together to overcome that fear and live each day knowing you have the Kingdom of Heaven at hand?

Notes:

Week 31

There's No Better Way – Obedience I

Usually when a father talks with his sons about obedience, it is not a pretty thing. The talk usually happens after the son has done something wrong and has to deal with the consequences of his actions. It may not be a gentle reminder because, I can tell you, the consequences from the father will be in proportion to the level of trust that is lost.

Then there is the opposite situation, where you have an opportunity to see the positive impacts of obedience. It may be a small or subtle occasion but one that you can point to that says, because the son obeys (translated trusts) the father, pain is avoided and a life is made richer. That happened recently on a trip to California. As my oldest son got prepared to go for a run in the countryside we had a discussion about bears. They were extremely active in the area and could be provoked if one was not careful. The conversation was what I would have expected, dad was overreacting and that of course the son knew best. When he returned he told the family that on the run he saw several bears. At one particular point in the run he was rounding a large rock that he could not see around. Remembering our conversation, he started clapping and, sure enough, a large bear had been on the other side. Hearing him clapping had made the bear run away, thus avoiding a nasty collision. Obedience in this case was a matter of trust, and relationship. It's the same with God, but the outcomes are much more vital and the benefits eternal.

- Walking Tall
- Got Spirit?
- Letting go.
- You can't pick and choose.
- Reaping the reward or paying the price.

Challenge:

Men: Discuss with your young man the concepts of loving obedience and the benefits it can have in your relationships, both with you and with God. Help him to understand that a conscious obedience can bring joy and peace.

Young Men: Think of areas in your life where you struggle with obedience, both with your parents and with God. Challenge yourself to work towards an obedient spirit that shows you trust God's will for your life.

There's No Better Way – Obedience I

Monday

Verse: 2 John 6

> *And this is love: that we walk in obedience to his commands. As you have heard from the beginning, his command is that you walk in love.*

Father's Thoughts: True love through obedience is putting action to your words. Walking in obedience means more than just not doing bad things; it means you actively DO the right things. Walking in love means you get off your tail, get out there and do something for someone who desperately needs you. Like any good thing in life, this takes forethought, planning, and ACTION.

Sons' Thoughts: Love is something that is kind of taboo in the world that we live in today. Sure, we hear all about "the power of love" and other petty phrases like that, but we are pressed to find somebody actually carrying out acts of love. Here in 2 John, God is telling us that love *is* obedience. We can show our parents, our siblings, and other people that we love them simply by obeying them.

Discussion Questions: What are you doing for the Kingdom of God? When was the last time you got out and helped someone who needed help, talked to someone who was lonely? What can you do this week to begin walking in obedience?

Notes: _____
_____
_____
_____

Tuesday

Verse: Acts 5:32

> *We are witnesses of these things, and so is the Holy Spirit, whom God has given to those who obey him.*

Father's Thoughts: Obedience means not keeping your mouth shut. Don't be called as a hostile witness. Through obedience we are given such a great gift, the very Holy Spirit of God.

Sons' Thoughts: The Holy Spirit becomes part of us as we accept Christ, but what exactly does this mean? This means that we are no longer trying to make an impact for God on our own. We have God himself in the spirit form pushing us along during our personal struggles.

Discussion Questions: Why do you think that obedience is a requirement for our relationship to God? How does this give us the strength to tell others about Him?

Notes: _____
_____
_____
_____

Wednesday

Verse: Genesis 22:12

> *"Do not lay a hand on the boy," He said. "Do not do anything to him. Now I know that you fear God, because you have not withheld from me your son, your only son."*

Father's Thoughts: Obedience will mean tough choices. We must have confidence that in our obedience, God will direct our paths even when we cannot see what is around the corner. The key is to move forward; it is easier to turn a moving car than one standing still.

Sons' Thoughts: As a teenager who is not quite ready to have children of my own, I cannot fully understand Abraham's struggle here, but I know how much my father loves me, and for him to even think about doing what God asked Abraham to do here would show a faith in God that I really look up to.

Discussion Questions: Have you had to make some tough choices? Are you confident that God will direct you in those choices? What are ways that you can work at better knowing and following God's directions?

Notes: _____
_____
_____
_____

Thursday

Verse: Matthew 23: 23

> *Woe to you, teachers of the law and Pharisees, you hypocrites! You give a tenth of your spices—mint, dill and cumin. But you have neglected the more important matters of the law—justice, mercy and faithfulness. You should have practiced the latter, without neglecting the former.*

Father's Thoughts: You cannot pick and choose your areas of obedience to fit your own personal agenda. Do not follow Thomas Jefferson's example and rip out the parts of the Bible that he did not like.

Sons' Thoughts: This is an example of religion vs. relationship. We can go to church 3 times per week, read our Bible at least 20 minutes a day, say all the right things, and sing all of the right songs, and it can all mean absolutely nothing. The problem with the Pharisees was their pride. Those guys thought that they were better than everybody else because they knew a lot of Bible verses. Too bad they didn't live the verses out.

Discussion Questions: What areas do you feel that you handle best in following Christ? What areas cause you problems?

Notes: _____
_____
_____
_____

Friday

Verse: Isaiah 1: 18-20

> *"Come now, let us reason together," says the LORD.*
> *"Though your sins are like scarlet, they shall be as white as snow;*
> *though they are red as crimson, they shall be like wool.*
> *If you are willing and obedient, you will eat the best from the land;*
> *but if you resist and rebel, you will be devoured by the sword."*
> *For the mouth of the LORD has spoken.*

Father's Thoughts: Obedience has its rewards, rebellion it price. Every son of a father who fairly disciplines knows this lesson. Whenever I have talked to men who have lost their way, one of the common themes that I hear are either a poor relationship with their father or none at all. That is a mirror for our relationship to God. We must stay connected with him and learn to obey him and he will help us to put sin and rebellion behind us.

Sons' Thoughts: God lays it out pretty simply here in this verse. Resist and rebel, get devoured by the sword. Not a very pleasant way to go about living. As we're growing up there will always be the urge to rebel against our parents. But I have learned along the way, much like our Lord, our parents love us and always want the best for us.

Discussion Questions: What is your greatest argument as father and son? How do you deal with it on a daily basis? How does that reflect on how God treats, discipline, rebellion and obedience?

Notes: _____

_____

_____

_____

Week 32

To be Happy in Jesus – Obedience II

Earlier we talked about obedience requiring action. Action, by its very nature involves risk. When Christ talked with his disciples about obedience, He meant going all the way regardless of obstacles or the sacrifice involved. This must have been why Jesus called the type of men that he did as apostles. These were not weak men; they were fishermen, business owners and zealots. These were the type of men that when faced with tough choices in the future would take the necessary steps to take the message of the Good News forward.

Jesus called men like Paul, a man's man who survived stoning, beatings, shipwrecks and jail, all in the act of obedience. Another one of Jesus' followers, Matthew, also known as Levi, was a rich and successful thug (translated tax collector). He was a very unlikely disciple but God called him to obedience, which meant leaving a very high- rolling lifestyle and obeying Christ's call. Because of his obedience we have the unique gospel of Matthew, a detailed eyewitness account of Christ's ministry. If these men were not tough in their obedience, who would have ever listened to them? So where are you on the tough/obedience meter?

- The life you save may be your own.
- The give and the take.
- The world's toll booth

- The risk of obeying
- Time for a change

Challenge:

Men: Discuss the realities of obedience to Christ. Talk about the changes that will be required that will make you stand out to the world.

Young Men: Think of the things that you have to risk in obeying God and living for Christ. Resolve to be the type of man that your peers will respect and listen to as they see the strength you display in following Christ.

To be Happy in Jesus – Obedience II

Monday

Verse: Luke 9:23

> *Then he said to them all: "If anyone would come after me, he must deny himself and take up his cross daily and follow me.*

Father's Thoughts: Obedience will mean sacrifice. For a young man, that might mean you have to tell your friends that you have to 'pass' on certain activities. It can be very hard to say no to something that on the surface looks exciting, inviting, and safe while underneath it can be damaging. This is a daily situation. Temptation doesn't take a day off and it never leaves you alone. You don't have to face this alone.

Sons' Thoughts: This means that walking with Christ is definitely not going to be easy. Carrying a cross was very hard work, as will be living a Christ-like lifestyle. Life during middle school and high school are hard enough, but living a truly faithful life is going to be a constant struggle.

Discussion Questions: How can your brothers in Christ help you to face daily trials and temptations? What do you feel you need to sacrifice to Him?

Notes: _____
_____
_____
_____

Tuesday

Verse: Luke 9:24

For whoever wants to save his life will lose it, but whoever loses his life for me will save it.

Father's Thoughts: Have you ever given something away only to find it come right back to you? I observed on Christmas morning the way you approached the gifts given to you. If you sat in the corner and played with your gifts you soon got bored and didn't get much out of it. If you 'gave it away' by sharing it with someone else, you enjoyed it twice as much and much longer. When you obey Christ and give your life away, you actually gain more. You gain both fellowship and eternal life.

Sons' Thoughts: This is the ultimate challenge of trust right here. As a student, I like everything to be under my control. I like things to be exactly as I plan them, but we have to learn to trust God in a way that your entire life becomes His, living the way that He would want us to rather than what we want.

Discussion Questions: What part of your life have you been hording, what part do you need to lose, give away?

Notes: _____
_____
_____
_____

Wednesday

Verse: Luke 9:25

> *What good is it for a man to gain the whole world, and yet lose or forfeit his very self?*

Father's Thoughts: Obedience will require tradeoffs in many aspects of our life. A friend of mine in high school thought he could take a shortcut to making it rich. But the morphine that he sold soon made its way into his own body and before my eyes he turned from a funny and talented teenager into a mere ghost of himself. When the police raided the school one spring, my friend lost everything, including his freedom.

Sons' Thoughts: Have you ever known a friend who all of a sudden got a job and you felt that he completely disappeared from you and your friends' lives? Usually those people are miserable. They have forsaken their life just to make money, believing that this will make him happy. Obey God when he says that you will lose yourself if you try to find fulfillment in the world rather than in Him.

Discussion Questions: Why is the toll of worldly things our very self, our soul?

Notes: _____
_____
_____
_____

Thursday

Verse: Luke 9:26

> *If anyone is ashamed of me and my words, the Son of Man will be ashamed of him when he comes in his glory and in the glory of the Father and of the holy angels.*

Father's Thoughts: Obeying God takes boldness. If a man really believes in something or in someone, does he not stand up for that idea or person? When someone insults your best friend you take up for them, you fight for them.

Sons' Thoughts: As Christians, we are going to be made fun of, and even if it is behind our backs it still hurts. This is the true test when it comes to standing up for God. We need to be proud of our God and all that He has done for us rather than deny Him for worldly gain.

Discussion Questions: Are you willing to stand up and be counted for Christ? Will you obey him with a bold stand, or will you hang your head in silent disobedience?

Notes: _____
_____
_____
_____

Friday

Verse: Romans 7:17-18

> *But thanks be to God that, though you used to be slaves to sin, you wholeheartedly obeyed the form of teaching to which you were entrusted. You have been set free from sin and have become slaves to righteousness.*

Father's Thoughts: With obedience comes transformation. One important transformation is the thought of who we belong to. If we have given ourselves up to sin then it will control our lives, it will create negative consequences that we have to face all our lives. If we give up control to God's righteousness, it will create positive consequences like confidence, a clear conscience, and a love for others that we will have the rest of our lives, and beyond.

Sons' Thoughts: The word slave brings all sorts of bad connotations with it. But think about being a slave to righteousness. Everything that you do is governed by what is right and true.

Discussion Questions: What are some of the consequences you have faced when you have sinned? How can you overcome these by giving all up to Christ?

Notes: _____
_____
_____
_____

Week 33

But to Trust and Obey – Obedience III

When you talk about the men who followed Christ, you don't have to dig very far to get a sense of what they gave up to follow Him. Every one of them had to give up something dear to become the men who would take the Word to the ends of the earth. Some gave up successful careers; others went from following one teacher (John the Baptist) to follow Jesus. Even others gave up their political activities to obey Christ's call. The things that you are asked to give up may be small or they may be large. It could be a personal relationship that you need to walk away from because it is causing you to live outside of God's will. It could be a job that you need to give up because it is causing you to stray from God's perfect will in your life.

You are a collection of all your experiences. Everything that you do, everything that you are can be used for the Kingdom of God. Examine your past, your present, your motives, your gifts and your desires. These are gifts you have been given to prepare you for obedience. Things that take you away from that obedience will only weigh you down. This does not mean you walk away from your responsibilities, for these are also gifts from God, but you need to examine them in light of your calling and make sure they are really responsibilities and not excuses.

- The commitment.
- The reality.
- The excuse.
- Stirring the waters.
- The best example

Challenge:

Men: Create a 'life map' and discuss it with your young man. Map out how you have come to this point in your life, what decisions you have made along the way and how they have brought you closer to God. Discuss those decisions that may have taken you away from God as well.

Young Men: Start your own life map. You are never too young to have "a story". Begin to map out where you want to go and discuss obstacles that might get in your way.

But to Trust and Obey – Obedience III

Monday

Verse: Luke 9:57

> *As they were walking along the road, a man said to him, "I will follow you wherever you go."*

Father's Thoughts: You are entering a very exciting time of your life. You are beginning to make the choices of if and where you will go to school after you graduate high school, what profession you might pursue. Even in early high school years you will make decisions that can affect your future by what classes you take, what clubs you join, and the friends you make.

Sons' Thoughts: Saying this to Jesus is basically saying "I'm giving up my entire life and everything that is in it to follow you and your teachings." This is the attitude that we should have when we follow Jesus.

Discussion Questions: Think about the way you follow Christ. Will you be called to follow him in a full-time vocation through ministry or missions? Will you be called to be a witnessing lay person? What will be your path to follow him?

Notes: _____
_____
_____
_____

Tuesday

Verse: Luke 9:58

> *Jesus replied, "Foxes have holes and birds of the air have nests, but the Son of Man has no place to lay his head."*

Father's Thoughts: Obedience to God's call will entail certain choices and risks. The bold man that said "I will follow you wherever you go" obviously needed to understand that. He needed to know what he was getting himself into, so Jesus let him know that it would not be an easy road. Maybe in the man's heart he was only looking for a comfortable or protective group to hang out with, like some young people feel in joining gangs.

Sons' Thoughts: This kind of lifestyle is going to be rough. There might be times when you feel alone in the world, but God will always be there.

Discussion Questions: As you chose how to obey God's call in your life, are you going in with your eyes open and your heart set willing to take the risks, make the sacrifices?

Notes: _____
_____
_____
_____

Wednesday

Verse: Luke 9:59-60

> *He said to another man, "Follow me." But the man replied, "Lord, first let me go and bury my father." Jesus said to him, "Let the dead bury their own dead, but you go and proclaim the kingdom of God."*

Father's Thoughts: Excuses, excuses. Some people will call them reasons but we all know an excuse when we hear one. I heard someone explain that the terminology used did not mean that the man's father was lying dead at his home and had to be buried that day. It meant that he would stay at home until his father eventually died and when it was convenient and he no longer had any earthly obligations, then he would follow Christ.

Sons' Thoughts: God HAS to be the number one priority in our life. Look at what you hold most dear to you and examine whether God is the most important thing in your life. If not, try to switch whatever that thing is into something that you can use to proclaim the Kingdom of God.

Discussion Questions: Should we obey Christ only when it is convenient for us?

Notes: _____
_____
_____
_____

Thursday

Verse: Luke 9:61-62

> *Still another said, "I will follow you, Lord; but first let me go back and say good-by to my family." Jesus replied, "No one who puts his hand to the plow and looks back is fit for service in the kingdom of God."*

Father's Thoughts: God doesn't want us to hurt our relationships or our love for our families. He wants us to put in perspective our earthly obligations versus our heavenly ones. As your father, I do not want to stand in the way of your following God's will for your life. You should be focused on obeying Him first. Hey, it doesn't mean I won't challenge you on your choices for your life or try to provide guidance, it just means that in the end, you must be obedient to God's call.

Sons' Thoughts: God still wants us to work hard, make good grades and be the best athlete that we can, but he does not want these things to override our relationship with Him.

Discussion Questions: Are you willing to boldly follow God's will for your life even if that means stirring the waters at home?

Notes: _____
_____
_____
_____

Friday

Verse: Hebrews 5:7-9

> *During the days of Jesus' life on earth, he offered up prayers and petitions with loud cries and tears to the one who could save him from death, and he was heard because of his reverent submission. Although he was a son, he learned obedience from what he suffered and, once made perfect, he became the source of eternal salvation for all who obey him.*

Father's Thoughts: Can we have a better example of the power of prayer than to see how Jesus Himself thought it was so vitally important? Jesus showed us that building a humble relationship with the Father is the source of our strength in all times and all circumstances.

Sons' Thoughts: We learn by trial and error sometimes. When we are little, we are constantly being reprimanded for things that we did not know were wrong. It is through our own experiences that we can find out for ourselves what God wants us to do and how He wants us to do it.

Discussion Questions: Discuss both of your approaches to prayer. Do you set aside time to pray and to meditate on God's word?

Notes: _____
_____
_____
_____

Week 34

What are You Lookin' at – The Sex talk

—⚏—

So this is the week we have "that" talk. I guess the normal expectation is that the sex talk from a Christian perspective would be filled with a long list of don'ts. Well, there are a few: <u>Do not commit adultery</u> and Jesus' clarity of <u>Don't even lust in your heart</u>. These really cover so many things including a pretty sharp ban on all sex outside of marriage and the fact that purity is a high standard. That is a great start.

My take on sex is to focus on the Do's.

- Do respect women, starting with your mother and sisters. This respect needs to be both physical and spiritual.
- Do begin early studying the ideal traits of a Christian woman and seek these out in your dating relationships. It is amazing how much less temptation you end up with when you are both seeking God's will.
- Do start off your dating life with a resolution to keep things healthy and safe. Choose who you date and where you date very carefully. Creating a relationship with her parents is a good first step.
- Do start by looking at yourself and asking, "Am I being an example of a strong, kind and loving Christian young man?"

- Do plan your time with your dates in such a way that you avoid temptation rather than rely on willpower.
- I don't want to be alone.
- You are in this together.
- RUN
- Don't take that second look.
- Set up the ideal.

Challenge:

Men: Be open with your young man about the struggles that all men have with sexual matters. Resolve to become a team that can discuss these issues openly and resolve to teach healthy relationships with women.

Young Men: Don't hesitate to discuss sexual issues with your father. Believe me, they have dealt with all of the things that you have or will face. Form a bond of trust that will allow you to be honest, even when things do not go well.

What are You Lookin' at – The Sex talk

Monday

Verse: Genesis 2:18

> *The LORD God said, "It is not good for the man to be alone. I will make a helper suitable for him."*

Father's Thoughts: God wasn't talking about Bob the handyman here. God recognized our need for companionship, our need to be intimate, to be loved. He did not say, "let's make him a servant," No, he provided a helper, which means we are in need of help. Suitable? Men need a helper that both complement and fulfill him, one that shares his hopes and his dreams and one that will share his love of God.

Sons' Thoughts: We are relational beings, and without human interaction, we become weak. We constantly need feedback to how we are living life and friendship is something that even Jesus needed.

Discussion Questions: Who is that helper suitable for you? Who is that woman that will both complement and fulfill you? Are you confident in a God who will provide?

Notes: _____
_____
_____
_____

Tuesday

Verse: Genesis 2:24

> *For this reason a man will leave his father and mother and be united to his wife, and they will become one flesh.*

Father's Thoughts: Independence is a funny thing. With it comes great responsibility. When God provides you with a "helper suitable for' you, it will be a marker in your life, a time to stand on your own, to step out together and take on the responsibility of marriage and become a new family. Becoming 'one flesh' is so much more than a sexual description, it means you intertwine all aspects of your life together, physical, mental and spiritual.

Sons' Thoughts: Marriage is the perfect metaphor for our relationship with God. He loves us unconditionally, and as you begin to understand another human being, you begin to see things in the same way. If you were to give your wife 2 hours every Sunday, and 10 minutes every morning, that relationship would be very strained. In the same way that you love a human, love and cherish your relationship with God.

Discussion Questions: When you hear the phrase 'one flesh,' what does it mean to you?

Notes: _____
_____
_____
_____

Wednesday

Verse: 1 Corinthians 6:18

> *Flee from sexual immorality. All other sins a man commits are outside his body, but he who sins sexually sins against his own body.*

Father's Thoughts: I like the use of the word 'flee' in this passage. RUN, GET OUT OF THERE, BACK AWAY, NOW! Part of being sexually responsible is making sure that you avoid situations that could cause temptation. There will be times that you inadvertently find yourself in the wrong place at the wrong time. Flee. Be a man, be a leader, grab her hand and leave. She will respect and admire you for it. Do you have enough respect of your own body to get out of there?

Sons' Thoughts: Everybody has been in an "iffy" situation. Maybe it is alone with your girlfriend or at a party or dance where we know we should not be. The best way to avoid sexual immorality is to avoid any situation where a temptation might arise.

Discussion Questions: Do you have enough respect for your own body to get out of there?

Notes: _____
_____
_____
_____

Thursday

Verse: 2 Samuel 11:2-5

> *One evening David got up from his bed and walked around on the roof of the palace. From the roof he saw a woman bathing. The woman was very beautiful, and David sent someone to find out about her. The man said, "Isn't this Bathsheba, the daughter of Eliam and the wife of Uriah the Hittite?" Then David sent messengers to get her. She came to him, and he slept with her. (She had purified herself from her uncleanness.) Then she went back home. The woman conceived and sent word to David, saying, "I am pregnant."*

Father's Thoughts: Let me get straight to the point. YOU WILL BE SEXUALLY TEMPTED. You are a man, God gave you sexual desire. It is both a gift and a burden. David took that gift and made it a burden. He had many chances to turn away but he pursued it, going out of his way to turn good into bad. He could have turned away from the window, but he kept looking. After looking, he sent someone out to find out about the woman. After he found out she was married, he could have said, "oh well," and dropped it.

Sons' Thoughts: Not only will you be tempted, there will be people who will try to tempt you. Did Bathsheba know that David was up there watching her? Maybe, but it doesn't matter. You are still responsible for your actions. David acted on his temptations and this led straight to sexual immorality and loads of guilt and separation from God.

Discussion Questions: As a man, and a man of God, can you break the temptation cycle and dedicate yourself to sexual purity?

Notes: _____
_____
_____
_____

Friday

Verse: I Corinthians 13:4-7

> *Love is patient, love is kind. It does not envy, it does not boast, it is not proud. It is not rude, it is not self-seeking, it is not easily angered, it keeps no record of wrongs. Love does not delight in evil but rejoices with the truth. It always protects, always trusts, always hopes, always perseveres.*

Father's Thoughts: Do you want to do what is right? Then look to the ideal. If you truly know what love is, then you will have in your heart the means to avoid sexual temptation.

Sons' Thoughts: When you are in a relationship with someone, take a long look at it and see if these characteristics are present. Are you patient with one another? Are you kind? Can you trust one another, and so on?

Discussion Questions: Take a pencil and do this exercise: Write down the ideal traits of the woman that you might want to spend the rest of your life married to. Great, now write down all the traits that you have that might attract that "right woman" to you. Was a fervent ability to love one of your traits…..think about it, pray about it. God, how can I be the best at loving the woman of my dreams?

Notes: _____
_____
_____
_____

Week 35

R.E.S.P.E.C.T. — Respecting Others

One of the most commonly used ice-breakers is to have each member of a group tell something about themselves that no one else would know about the teller. The results can be fascinating. Some adults you know have done some pretty amazing things that would give you a tremendous amount of respect if you took the time to know their stories. It is strange that in a Christian setting, people are often most reluctant to reveal who they truly are, or what they have done in life, maybe afraid that people will be judgmental.

The story that I like to tell is…..well, yes, I dated a princess. The relationship did not last long, it did not have a fairy tale ending, but for a brief moment as a sophomore in high school, I really 'went out with' a princess. Details? OK. My father, an amateur radio operator –a ham— had a convention in Malaysia to which he took my mother and me. The host was a prince of the Malaysian state of Johor. He had three kids, a son and two daughters, all three close to me in age. I was the only other teenager there and the four of us ran around together playing practical jokes and having a great time and one of the princesses and I hit it off. Yes, there was a royal kiss involved, hey, we were teenagers. For that brief point in time, we were all equals, regardless of their royal, and my 'common' standing and the fact that we had very little in common. As Christians, we do have something in common: the love and salvation of our Lord Jesus Christ. He took those nails, bore that cross for all of us. Regardless of "station" we should then respect each other as brothers and sisters, equals, sharing a common gift.

> Be consistent in how you treat others.
> - Love them as much as you love yourself.
>
> Do you really love and honor those around you?
> - Starting with the heart
>
> We have a big job to do.
> - Working at it together
>
> Hey, what's in it for me?
> - Ummm, is that really what's important?
>
> Is it Live and Let Live?
> - Or Live and Forgive?

Challenge:
Men: As your son gets older and more mature, openly discuss your path and the path other men have taken to Christ. Help them to respect others' 'stories.'

Young Men: Learn to treat others with the respect they deserve. Understand that each one of us as Christians have walked a path, sometimes rocky, to get where we are today.

R.E.S.P.E.C.T. — Respecting Others

Monday

Verse: James 2:8-9

> *If you really keep the royal law found in Scripture, "Love your neighbor as yourself," you are doing right. But if you show favoritism, you sin and are convicted by the law as lawbreakers.*

Father's Thoughts: Respecting others is a matter of consistency. I know it is natural in school to run with a certain group. They might have something in common with you such as a sport, or activity, or lifestyle. That in itself is not a problem. James unlocks the key. Love them like you love yourself, and treat them as you want to be treated. Respect others through God's love.

Sons' Thoughts: Think about how much we actually love ourselves. Compare the time that we spend thinking about ourselves and then think about how much time we spend thinking about how we could help out others. This is how much God wants us to love others. He wants us to love others as much as we love ourselves.

Discussion Questions: What happens when you meet someone from outside the group of friends that you run around with? Do you treat them differently or badly because they are not like you?

Notes: _____
_____
_____
_____

Tuesday

Verse: Romans 12:9-10

> *Love must be sincere. Hate what is evil; cling to what is good. Be devoted to one another in brotherly love. Honor one another above yourselves.*

Father's Thoughts: Respect starts with love, love leads to devotion and devotion leads to honor. We live in a time where we are bombarded with encouragement to look out for number one. We see that on the athletic fields, in the movies and every magazine screams out "what's in it for me." God wants us to move past that, to put others first and respect his children above our selfish desires.

Sons' Thoughts: Sincerity is very important when it comes to love. To love somebody, we have to be completely honest with them. The idea of brotherly love holds the same concept as well. You have to help each other strive for good and let the devotion for good spill into your friendships.

Discussion Questions: What is your best quality or skill? How did you get it? Pick five people you know and discuss what they do best. Do you always look at someone and think of what they do better than you? Do you respect them for it?

Notes: _____
_____
_____
_____

Wednesday

Verse: Philippians 2:1-2

> *If you have any encouragement from being united with Christ, if any comfort from his love, if any fellowship with the Spirit, if any tenderness and compassion, then make my joy complete by being like-minded, having the same love, being one in spirit and purpose.*

Father's Thoughts: One of the ways you can respect others is by knowing your own purpose. If you know where you are going, if you are confident in your own path, then it is much easier to then grab the hands of others and bring them along. Look around you. The people who have the most problems, the ones who are self destructive tend to be those who have no purpose, have no direction and have no confidence in themselves. Seek what God has for you, his perfect will, and in that confidence you will take others there with you.

Sons' Thoughts: The idea of blending spirit and purpose is the idea that we need to put our faith into practice in real life situations. We can have a tender heart but have a hard time using it when the stakes are high. God wants us to trust in Him in the real world by doing what He wants us to do and not be timid.

Discussion Questions: What do you think your purpose is as a Christian man? Have you discussed this with those who are closest to you?

Notes: _____
_____
_____
_____

Thursday

Verse: Philippians 2:3-4

Do nothing out of selfish ambition or vain conceit, but in humility consider others better than yourselves. Each of you should look not only to your own interests, but also to the interests of others.

Father's Thoughts: I used to have a boss that we said lived in a two- by- two- by -six foot box. Basically, if it did not affect him personally, he could not care less. The problem is, two- by –two- by -six foot boxes strangely resemble coffins. God sets a pretty high standard on how we treat others. We may not always live up to those standards but if we will get outside our own box, it's a good start.

Sons' Thoughts: The competitive world that we all grew up in has taught us to try our hardest to be the best there is, and there is nothing wrong with that unless this means that we believe we are inherently better than other people. Some people may have been born with different talents, but this does not make us better in God's eyes than anyone else.

Discussion Questions: What are some practical ways you can learn more about those around you? How can you help others reach their goals, fulfill their dreams?

Notes: _____
_____
_____

Friday

Verse: Colossians 3:12-13

> *Therefore, as God's chosen people, holy and dearly loved, clothe yourselves with compassion, kindness, humility, gentleness and patience. Bear with each other and forgive whatever grievances you may have against one another. Forgive as the Lord forgave you.*

Fathers Thoughts: How do we respect others? Getting dressed doesn't mean we hold our clothes in our arms and put on only the articles we want, only when we feel like it. We get fully clothed. These qualities are something we should strive for as Christians and will ensure that we respect others. But forgiveness holds a special place in God's heart. He was willing to give his son Jesus to forgive us. We need to be willing to forgive others and put real meat to our respect.

Sons' Thoughts: These are what God has set apart to tell us how we should act: We should be compassionate, humble, gentle, and patient. We should forgive others of what we are holding between us. These are the things that God specifically laid out for us to be, so we should strive to let these characteristics become part of us.

Discussion Questions: What is the worst thing that anyone has ever done to you? Have you forgiven that person? What makes it hard to forgive and can the two of you work together to find a solution?

Notes: _____
_____
_____
_____

Week 36

We're All in This Together - Fellowship

I remember like it was today the potluck suppers we used to have at our church in Taiwan (for those under the age of 40, potlucks are a buffet of homemade food – never micro waved). Because we were such a diverse congregation, we were treated to such fantastic dishes of Asian, American and European cuisine. The food was great, but the talk was better. It was such a relaxing time where we got to know each other by building friendships, friendships that would go with us the rest of the week, to school and in the neighborhoods, to the teen club at the local U.S. military base and beyond.

Lately, I have renewed a similar type of fellowship, our Thursday morning men's Bible study. While we drink coffee and munch on bagels, we share the same type of close friendships where we share our innermost thoughts, our fears and our triumphs. We pray for each other, challenge each other and hold each other accountable. The boys have had similar groups called Life Groups. The closeness that has evolved from these meetings is evident and has led not only to deeper friendships, but to opportunities for missions and leadership.

I have heard men say that they can worship God anywhere; they do not need to be in "organized" religious activities. It is true that worship does not require a specific place, but God gave us "the Church," not as a building, but as a community of believers, strengthening each other. As men, we are stronger together, in church, and out.

- Can we just get along?
- What a machine
- Don't let it get away
- Strength in numbers
- Men of steel

Challenge:

Men: Discuss with your young men and show them with your life and relationships the value of fellowship with fellow believers, especially with other Christian men.

Young Men: Strive to build strong friendships based on a mutual relationship with Christ. Strive to be active in your church or in other groups that bind together to spread the Good News and strengthen those around you everyday.

We're All in This Together - Fellowship

Monday

Verse: 1 Corinthians 1:10-11

> *I appeal to you, brothers, in the name of our Lord Jesus Christ, that all of you agree with one another so that there may be no divisions among you and that you may be perfectly united in mind and thought. My brothers, some from Chloe's household have informed me that there are quarrels among you.*

Father's Thoughts: One of the signs of youth are raging hormones. Young men can find themselves in the middle of confrontations and not even know how they got there. This is not unique to adolescence. There are situations everyday that can lead to conflict. God calls us to be peacemakers within His church, to rise above the day- to -day annoyances and work to find common ground. We have enough enemies outside the church trying to bring us down, so let's avoid friction on the inside that can open us up to pain.

Sons' Thoughts: Have you ever watched the Tour de France? If so, you might have realized how much of a team sport cycling really is. The team leader is only as good as those who can help him up the hills, get him food and water, and keep him out of trouble. This parallels our spiritual walk. Trying to live a godly life on our own is like trying to win the Tour de France without a team. It is impossible.

Discussion Questions: What are some common issues that you have noticed that can cause quarrels in the church? How can you as a young man be a peacemaker?

Notes: _____
_____
_____
_____

Tuesday

Verse: 1 Corinthians 12:12

> *The body is a unit, though it is made up of many parts; and though all its parts are many, they form one body. So it is with Christ.*

Father's Thoughts: Recognize the unique qualities in those around you, especially those your age. The church is a collection of many people, each with gifts and talents. What a great opportunity to work together as a unit.

Sons' Thoughts: Some are made to talk, some are made to listen, some are sent out to mission fields, and some are asked to restock the pencils in the aisles. We all make up the body of Christ and every job is important, no matter how small and insignificant it seems.

Discussion Questions: What talents do you think you have? What are one or two practical ways you can use them for the cause of Christ?

Notes: _____
_____
_____
_____

Wednesday

Verse: Hebrews 10:25

> *Let us not give up meeting together, as some are in the habit of doing, but let us encourage one another—and all the more as you see the Day approaching.*

Father's Thoughts: I have often heard the excuse, 'I don't need to go to church, I can worship wherever I am'. This is true, but the purpose of the church is not just worship, it is the combining of our strengths and gifts to work together for God's glory. When you leave this out it is easy to get discouraged. Remember, the predator does not attack the pack, he looks for the weak stray.

Sons' Thoughts: When people become isolated, they begin to read into things too much. We are relational beings, and we need feedback from other people. Plus, if God reveals something to us, we need to share it with others.

Discussion Questions: What are ways you can strengthen your fellowship with other Christians? What opportunities do you have to use your gifts and talents in conjunction with others?

Notes: _____
_____
_____
_____

Thursday

Verse: Ecclesiastes 4:12

> *Though one may be overpowered, two can defend themselves. A cord of three strands is not quickly broken.*

Father's Thoughts: What is the value of a few good friends? It is enormous. You should begin at a young age picking good friends who have a heart for the Lord. Be willing to stand together against the temptations and challenges that life will bring your way and together you will be stronger.

Sons' Thoughts: Standing against temptation is a lot harder when your friends are not standing there next to you helping you resist. We need to rely on one another and not get isolated in tough situations.

Discussion Questions: Who are your best friends? Do they provide you strength, do they help to build you up and to point you towards Christ and His righteousness? How can you be that kind of friend to others?

Notes: _____
_____
_____
_____

Friday

Verse: Proverbs 27:17

As iron sharpens iron, so one man sharpens another.

Father's Thoughts: One of the most influential men in my walk with Christ is a man that I argued with vehemently. Yet through those discussions, arguments and disagreements, we both became stronger in the Lord.

Sons' Thoughts: If you have a great idea about an invention that will help out humanity, you would not sit on it and hold it all to yourself. You would tell somebody, maybe everybody that you meet. It should be this way with God. You can share your ideas with others and they can share their ideas with you and you both become stronger and better.

Discussion Questions: Who challenges you the most in a strong but positive way? Are you willing to strengthen your relationships to a point where you can have strong life -changing conversations based on a love of God?

Notes: _____
_____
_____
_____

Week 37

Trust Me? No, Trust Him

I am sure that most of the world watched the Olympics in Beijing, my old hometown. China put on a great show but the best came in the pool. Michael Phelps was going for the most gold medals ever. If all of his golds had come from individual events, that in itself would have been amazing. To me the greatest accomplishment was the sweep in the relays. Yes, Phelps was the leader, yes, he was the best out there, but he had to trust in his teammates to pull him through. Some of the feats they accomplished were unbelievable. There were come-from-behind finishes, world records, and all the stuff of good drama.

In the end, Michael had to let go and trust his teammates. He had to let go and rely on them for their part. I do not know Michael's heart, but I can judge his actions and what I saw was marvelous. He not only trusted his teammates, he encouraged them and then made sure they got their own spotlight. How much more can we accomplish if we too can learn to trust. Not in man, for man will eventually fail us, but in a great sovereign God and His son Jesus Christ.

Not just any trust
- Trust that changes your attitude

All
- Not just for washing clothes

Who's afraid of......
- Well, anything.

You don't look scared
- Who is that big guy that's with you?

Maybe it's a tough request but,
- Never stop asking.

Challenge:
Men: Discuss areas of your life that you have had to turn over to God to get by. Share the accomplishments that you have that only came when you put your trust in Jesus.

Young Men: Give to God all the areas of your life that you are trying to run yourself. Learn to trust in His guidance. Make sure you are building your relationship with Him so you can be open to His teaching and leading.

Trust Me? No, Trust Him

Monday

Verse: Isaiah 25:9

> *In that day they will say, "Surely this is our God; we trusted in him, and he saved us. This is the Lord, we trusted in him; let us rejoice and be glad in his salvation.*

Father's Thoughts: What is the good of quiet trust? Are we afraid that people will think we are strange or radical by telling about what he has done in our lives? The fruits of trust, joy and salvation, are meant to be shared, they are meant to be given away and multiplied.

Sons' Thoughts: A key phrase here is rejoice and BE GLAD. Sometimes we may feel obligated to worship God or act in his name. God wants our lives to be rich and fulfilled, and the only way to achieve that is to put our trust in Him. Keep trusting.

Discussion Questions: Have you shared with anyone lately the joy that you have from trusting God?

Notes: _____
_____
_____
_____

Tuesday

Verse: Proverbs 3:5-6

Trust in the LORD with all your heart and lean not on your own understanding; in all your ways acknowledge him, and he will make your paths straight.

Father's Thoughts: Men have a tough time ever admitting we are wrong or that we don't know how to solve all the problems or challenges we face. We want to "lean on our own understanding" and appear perfect. It's a bad façade and can put us on some wickedly crooked paths.

Sons' Thoughts: Trusting in our Lord and Savior is not a half-hearted thing. It requires our entire focus and will-power. Let's crack this exterior shell of pride and replace it with one made with the hands of our maker. Keep trusting.

Discussion Questions: Are you willing to let go of your male ego and trust God with ALL your heart?

Notes: _____
_____
_____
_____

Wednesday

Verse: Psalms 56:4

> *In God, whose word I praise, in God I trust; I will not be afraid. What can mortal man do to me?*

Father's Thoughts: What is the easiest way to get beat? Convincing yourself you cannot win. Self-fulfilling defeatism is a cancer that can bring talented men to their knees. God tells us, almost screams at us at times through His word, HAVE CONFIDENCE!!! With our trust in Him there is nothing that can take our soul from him. Yet so many times we live in fear, we are afraid to take risks, we sometimes fail to fail because we fail to try. By putting ourselves in God's hands, by truly trusting him, we can turn that around and have a self-fulfilling, winning spirit.

Sons' Thoughts: We are often afraid of what may happen when we take our stand for the Lord. I know from experience, it's a tough thing to do, which requires us to take a big step out into nothingness waiting for the outcome. But we must always keep our trust and confidence. They will never fail us. Keep trusting.

Discussion Questions: Where in your life do you not trust Him? Where have you lost confidence?

Notes: _____
_____
_____
_____

Thursday

Verse: Judges 6:12

> *When the angel of the Lord appeared to Gideon, he said, "The Lord is with you, mighty warrior."*

Father's Thoughts: The Lord is with you, swift runner. The Lord is with you, mighty wrestler. The Lord is with you, talented musician. The Lord is with you, math wizard. God knows who we are, what our talents are, what we have to offer him with our lives and gifts. What a boost these words must have been to Gideon as he was being asked to trust God before battle. Take these words to heart because God is speaking them to you as well.

Sons' Thoughts: The Lord is with you. It's sometimes hard for us to truly believe this, not being able to physically see, hear, or touch Him. But as our Christian walk progresses, we begin to understand the many ways our God can communicate His presence and His will for our lives. Keep trusting.

Discussion Questions: Are you ready to put your trust in Him, to give him your very best as he introduces you to daily and lifelong challenges?

Notes: _____
_____
_____
_____

Friday

Verse: Judges 6:36-40

> *Gideon said to God, "If you will save Israel by my hand as you have promised—look, I will place a wool fleece on the threshing floor. If there is dew only on the fleece and all the ground is dry, then I will know that you will save Israel by my hand, as you said" And that is what happened. Gideon rose early the next day; he squeezed the fleece and wrung out the dew—a bowlful of water. Then Gideon said to God, "Do not be angry with me. Let me make just one more request. Allow me one more test with the fleece. This time make the fleece dry and the ground covered with dew." Than night God did so. Only the fleece was dry; all the ground was covered with dew.*

Father's Thoughts: Why do you think Gideon needed so many signs? The answer might be elusive but we should all be grateful that God was so patient with him. Being young and inexperienced, this may be a good lesson for you; never stop asking questions, never stop asking for guidance or for help. There may be a point where you can take it too far and you might hear God say what sometimes I am tempted to say: "Because I said so!!" Nevertheless, learn to trust God after the questions have been answered. Better yet, learn to trust Him before the answers are given.

Sons' Thoughts: My pastor talked recently about how many times Christians are told that it is a sin to ask questions of God. He believed this wasn't true, that we must always delve further into what God wants for our lives, but all the while continuing to trust Him to provide us with the necessary answers, which sometimes may even be no answer at all. So don't be afraid to ask questions, merely KEEP TRUSTING.

Discussion Questions: What questions or pending decisions do you have that are so important that you are tempted to ask God for a sign? Are you willing to seek his guidance with perseverance?

Notes:

Week 38

Making Those Tough Choices

—⚊⚊—

When the boys were young my wife and I devised a system that we hoped would cut down on arguing. Instead of saying to the boys, "What do you want to eat?" we would limit the choices and instead say, "Do you want spaghetti or chicken?" It was amazing the difference it made in the overall peace of the household. Well, in life, it's just not that simple. Every day we are faced with so many choices that it is surprising that everyone is not at the point of a nervous breakdown.

When God gave man the freedom of choice, I think He knew, like I know as a parent, that kids, as well as adults, would struggle making the tough ones. Thanks be to God, He does not abandon us to our own devices. Part of the relationship that He has built with us through His Son Jesus is the desire he displays to be a part of our decision making. Given the chance He will guide us even when the way is tough and the end out of sight.

There will be times when you cannot see an end to your problems.
- Maybe you need some good help.

There will be times when many people will be telling you which way to go.
- There's only one voice worth listening to.

There will be times that you want to please everyone.
- Make sure God is first in line.

There will be times when choices come with inner conflict.
- Overcoming the wrong direction

There will be times when making the right choices requires maturity.
- Ready to eat some meat

Challenge:
Men: Share with your son some of the tough choices that you have had to make as a man. Show him how you relied on God to get to the other side of the challenge.

Young Men: Determine now, while you are young, to build a such a deep relationship with God through Jesus Christ that leads you to make your life's decisions in the center of His will.

Making Those Tough Choices

Monday

Verse: Romans 8:26

> *In the same way, the Spirit helps us in our weakness. We do not know what we ought to pray for, but the Spirit himself intercedes for us with groans that words cannot express.*

Father's Thoughts: There have been times in my life that I had no spiritual strength. I really did not have the words to say, to ask for forgiveness, for help or both. At these times I recognized more than ever what a great gift the Holy Spirit is. It's like having a friend standing up for you, like a parent lifting a child over a barrier, like having someone reach down with his hand and pull you up when you have been knocked down.

Sons' Thoughts: How many times do we find ourselves at a loss for words when it comes to praying? How amazing it is to think that we can have a conversation with the Almighty Creator of the universe? God does not want us to think that he is unapproachable. He wants us to speak with Him, share our troubles and weaknesses, and rely on Him to help us through these tough times.

Discussion Questions: Have you thanked God lately for His gift of the Holy Spirit?

Notes: _____
_____
_____
_____

Tuesday

Verse: Colossians 2:8

> *See to it that no one takes you captive through hollow and deceptive philosophy, which depends on human tradition and the basic principles of this world rather than on Christ.*

Father's Thoughts: Don't be fooled, Satan does not have a long tail and a pitchfork. He comes at you with subtlety and stealth. You will hear things that sound logical, that sound easy, that when told in a convincing and charismatic manner seem to make sense. Instead, measure everything against this: Christ crucified, a sacrifice for our sins, raised from the dead, offering the gift of eternal life through your belief in Him.

Sons' Thoughts: We hear it all the time - our pastors or parents telling us we need to be IN this world, not OF this world. We are daily faced with struggles to ignore the things the world tells us are important. But this statement is so true. We were born into this world to spread the love of Jesus Christ. Let's not get sidetracked by the things that hinder us from this goal.

Discussion Questions: How can you develop a "Christ filter" when confronted by the world's attractive philosophies?

Notes: _____
_____
_____
_____

Wednesday

Verse: Galatians 1:10

> *Am I now trying to win the approval of men, or of God? Or am I trying to please men? If I were still trying to please men, I would not be a servant of Christ.*

Father's Thoughts: As men we are often looking around to see who is watching us. It seems natural for us to seek the approval of others or to look for the pat on the back. Yet, as Christians, we should not live our lives for anyone but Christ. Some of our actions in His name may not be well received. We must be willing to risk rejection of man for God's nod of approval.

Sons' Thoughts: Something I personally struggle with is trying to be a "people pleaser." As humans, we enjoy the attention of others and long to feel as if we belong. But remember- with God, we will always be important. The approval of men is miniscule compared to that of our Creator.

Discussion Questions: Are you the type that needs the praise of others to feel important? How can this hold you back as you try to make tough decisions?

Notes: _____
_____
_____
_____

Thursday

Verse: Galatians 5:17

> *For the sinful nature desires what is contrary to the Spirit, and the Spirit what is contrary to sinful nature. They are in conflict with each other so that you do not do what you want.*

Father's Thoughts: Some people will justify behavior with the words, "I'm just human," or "Boys will be boys." Natural tendencies are not an excuse for disobeying God. It is a tough struggle that all men will have to face, and through Christ, overcome.

Sons' Thoughts: The struggle between our sin nature and the Holy Spirit is an ongoing battle. Many times what we WANT to do isn't the right thing for us. If we fight to set aside this human desire and follow the path God has laid for us, we will find satisfaction in all that we do.

Discussion Questions: What are those things that you naturally struggle with? Are there certain characteristics and faults that you fight with constantly? How can you give those things over to God and let Him help you to conquer them?

Notes: _____
_____
_____
_____

Friday

Verse: Hebrews 5:12-13

> *In fact, though by this time you ought to be teachers, you need someone to teach you the elementary truths of God's word all over again. You need milk, not solid food! Anyone who lives on milk, being still an infant, is not acquainted with the teaching about righteousness.*

Father's Thoughts: Part of manhood and maturity is being accountable for our actions. Accountability is a terrible, yet wonderful thing. As we make choices we have to understand that we are accountable, accountable to God. The word of God exposes our actions and our choices, whether they are for good or for evil.

Sons' Thoughts: Christianity is an ongoing learning process. We can't expect to know everything there is to know the minute we accept Christ into our lives. It's also not something that's done and then pushed aside. Once we are saved, we continue to strive to live a lifestyle worthy of our Savior.

Discussion Questions: Are you willing to step up and be accountable for your actions? When have you made bad choices and then tried to hide from the consequences? What are some good choices you have made?

Notes: _____
_____
_____
_____

Week 39

The Unexplained

There are some things that just cannot be explained. When I was in college the Baptist Student Union took twenty of us on a mission trip to Romania. This was back during the darkest times of Communist/Dictatorial rule and the country was in terrible economic turmoil. Our project was to visit a number of churches to encourage the young people there to be bold for Christ and become leaders in the church. Several young people there were our translators and guides.

After singing at one church we packed our bags and headed to the train station for a five-hour trip to the next city. When we started to get on the train it was so crowded that only about half of our group was able to board. Unfortunately for those of us left on the platform, our translator….and our tickets….were on that train. It had begun to snow so we were huddled under the small shelter on the platform. A young girl from the last church had gone with us to the train station and she was now the only one left with us, but she did not speak English. Without warning, she suddenly picked up two of our bags and walked about 50 feet down the platform, OUT INTO THE SNOW. I don't know why but I felt compelled to go with her. I could tell she was praying so I did not even try to communicate with her. As she stood there, another train pulled up two tracks over. The box car door opened and a man from inside yelled at the girl. He was a member of the church AND a train station master. He was able to help us along our way. If that girl had not walked the 50 feet into the cold snow, he would have never seen us. Her prayers and ours were answered.

- The end of the world is coming.
- What a way to be swept off your feet
- Between a rock and a dry place
- Lions to the left of me, jokers to the right
- Instead of analyzing, just enjoy.

Challenge:
Men: Convince your young man to keep his eyes open for the unexpected miracles that happen around us. Encourage him to read his Bible and learn more about our great and mighty God.

Young Men: Be open to those things that just cannot be explained away by a modern world that does not want to see God's work. Read your Old Testament and enjoy the gift of God's word and His mighty deeds.

The Unexplained

Monday

Verse: Revelation 8:1

> *When he opened the seventh seal, there was silence in heaven for about half an hour.*

Father's Thoughts: I really don't know what to expect at the end times. I know that God has a plan, but I admit, I am baffled by the book of Revelation. The comfort that I have is in my relationship with Jesus Christ. No matter if I live to see the end of the world, or die an old man (you might think I am old already, so older man), I know I can trust that He has it all together.

Sons' Thoughts: Revelation is an extremely interesting conclusion to the New Testament. With the account of the end of the world, there has to be some points of interest. It is easy to get worrisome or troubled by the terrible things God has in store for an unbelieving world. But trust in Him; He always fulfills His promises. Those who believe will spend eternity in Heaven with Him.

Discussion Questions: Do you ever worry about the events going on around the world? Discuss those things together; do you trust that God has those things under control? How?

Notes: _____
_____
_____
_____

Tuesday

Verse: 2 Kings 2:11

As they were walking along and talking together, suddenly a chariot of fire and horses of fire appeared and separated the two of them, and Elijah went up to heaven in a whirlwind.

Father's Thoughts: What a way to go, out in a blaze of glory. Quite a bit different than being 85, surrounded by friends and family or tragically cut down in youth due to an accident or illness. The fact is, every day we have on earth is precious. Being young, you probably don't put a lot of thought into the end of your life; instead, you are putting all of your energy into living for today. The distinguishing factor here is the common denominator needed for all of us: doing God's will. Elijah was a man of God, he had lived his life focused on God's will, had mentored a successor, and was ready to go.

Sons' Thoughts: Elijah is the only human being recorded to have been taken up into Heaven without facing a mortal death. Elijah had done the Lord's work, his journey was over. But our journey continues, and we must make the choice to waste the time given us on this earth or go out in a "chariot of fire".

Discussion Questions: Why do you think God chose to take Elijah in this spectacular way? Was it for him or for those watching and reading?

Notes: _____
_____
_____
_____

Wednesday

Verse: Numbers 20:8-11

> *"Take the staff, and you and your brother Aaron gather the assembly together. Speak to that rock before their eyes and it will pour out its water. You will bring water out of the rock for the community so they and their livestock can drink." So Moses took the staff from the Lord's presence, just as he commanded him. He and Aaron gathered the assembly together in front of the rock and Moses said to them, "Listen, you rebels, must we bring you water out of this rock?" Then Moses raised his arm and struck the rock twice with his staff. Water gushed out, and the community and their livestock drank.*

Father's Thoughts: God can perform miracles. We see it in the Bible and if we look around we can see it in our own lives and in the lives of other Christians. God wants us to acknowledge his strength and his power and wants us to approach His power with humility. This is where the man Moses made a big mistake. He knew God was going to perform a miracle and He made a big show of striking the rock and turning the attention of the people to himself instead of to God. We must always be sure to give God the glory for His power and strength.

Sons' Thoughts: Moses gets really frustrated with God and decides to take things into his own hands instead of doing what God tells him to do. By this point, Moses is pretty much fed up with everything that is going on. His people are complaining, and God is telling him to talk to rocks, but since he doesn't trust God here, God in turn does not trust him enough to let him lead his people once they make it into the Promised Land.

Discussion Questions: What do you see around you that points to the greatness of God? How can you make sure you give God the glory of what He has done in your life?

Notes:

Thursday

Verse: Daniel 6:22

> *My God sent his angel, and he shut the mouths of the lions. They have not hurt me, because I was found innocent in his sight. Nor have I ever done any wrong before you, O king."*

Father's Thoughts: Maybe we will recognize a miracle when it happens, maybe we will not, but you should always look for God's handiwork. Daniel was saved from the lions' den for a long-term purpose. During those times where we feel the Lord working in our lives we need to strive to look around and see what the long-term purpose might be. Daniel was a young man who kept his integrity, and in doing so, touched the heart of a king.

Sons' Thoughts: In this day and age, we believe miracles to be a thing of the past. But God has never stopped performing miracles. We just need to learn to keep our eyes open and recognize these miracles, because they will not always come in the form that we expect.

Discussion Questions: What unexplained workings have you seen in your own life? Is there a long-term purpose in your pursuit of God's will?

Notes: _____
_____
_____
_____

Friday

Verse: Proverbs 30:18-19

> *There are three things that are too amazing for me, four that I do not understand:*
> - *the way of an eagle in the sky,*
> - *the way of a snake on a rock,*
> - *the way of a ship on the high seas,*
> - *and the way of a man with a maiden.*

Father's Thoughts: We have gotten pretty smart in these modern times. Scientists and theorists have answers to just about everything; at least they think they do. I don't get out in nature as much as I used to or as much as I want to but I still love to marvel at what God has made. Sometimes we forget how complicated and planned even the simplest part of our world is. No matter how smart we are, we will never know all the mysteries of God's creation, but we can still be grateful.

Sons' Thoughts: Solomon here is marveling at the creations of God we see around us. We often do not realize the amazingly intricate details of the organisms that create our planet, and how much joy God must have found in creating an entire universe for Himself. And above all, he chose us as the ones to rule over it, vastly displaying His even deeper love for us.

Discussion Questions: What do you love the most about God's creation? What does that teach you about God?

Notes: _____
_____
_____

Week 40

Submission to God

How many high school or college players stand on the sideline and call the plays? That is what the coach is for. How many tuba players lead the band? None that I know of. I think that is what the director is for. I could go on and on with examples but I believe that for these and other groups to succeed there must be submission to leadership. In a world where bucking against authority is sometimes seen as a virtue, humbly submitting to authority is not always applauded because the rebel has often been glorified.

Maybe that is why the idea of submission to God is often a difficult one for men. There may be some that see it as a sign of weakness. But when we start learning the heart of God and start to take His lead, we begin to see, well, why He is God and we are not.

God really does want us to be successful.
- If he is along for the ride

If you want your prayers to be heard by God
- Speak them to him not everyone else.

There are a whole lot of distractions.
- Get your priorities right.

There are times when you really, really want to do something else.
- Would you rather be fish bait?

Take a good look
- On the other hand, maybe you should keep your eyes to yourself.

Challenge:

Men: Guide your young men in the ways you can give yourself up to God's leadership. Give them examples of how you have learned to prioritize your life so that He is first in your life.

Young Men: Discuss how you view authority. When have there been times that you have resisted leadership and how you handled situations where you had to deal with a leader. Examine what you need to do in your own life to submit to God's leadership.

Submission to God

Monday

Verse: 1 Samuel 18:14

In everything he did he had great success, because the Lord was with him.

Father's Thoughts: "Because" is one of those words we use and don't really think about very much. Sometimes a parent will say, "Because I told you so," and those may be fighting words. But "because" most clearly denotes "cause and effect".
Just turn the sentence around. BECAUSE the Lord was with David, he had great success. Before we start striving for success, we need to strive for closeness and fellowship with God.

Sons' Thoughts: Often times we forget that second phrase at the end of this verse. We think that our accomplishments are rewards of what we have done. But God is the one who provides us with the talents/health/ability to do all of this. Now don't get me wrong. By all means rejoice in your triumphs, but rejoice by giving thanks to the One who makes all things possible.

Discussion Questions: What are the things that you want most in life, and what are your greatest ambitions? How will drawing closer to God and submitting to His will help you achieve them?

Notes: _____
_____
_____
_____

Tuesday

Verse: Matthew 6:5-6

> *"And when you pray, do not be like the hypocrites, for they love to pray standing in the synagogues and on the street corners to be seen by men. I tell you the truth, they have received their reward in full. But when you pray, go into your room, close the door and pray to your Father, who is unseen. Then your Father, who sees what is done in secret, will reward you.*

Father's Thoughts: What am I like when no one is watching? Do I use elegant words to speak to God? Jesus pointed out the hypocrisy of those whose only religion is for show. The test of true submission is what we are like when it is only the two of us, God and me, talking it through and getting it done.

Sons' Thoughts: In this verse, Jesus says that the hypocrites have received their reward in full. They wanted to be seen by all the people as one who is ardent in their prayer, and yes, they succeeded in this goal. But he tells us that the ones who are truly rewarded by their Father in Heaven are those who do not flaunt their worship, but only do so in love for their God.

Discussion Questions: Do you ever show off? What are those things in your life that you are most proud of? How can you give those over to God for His work?

Notes: _____
_____
_____
_____

Wednesday

Verse: Joshua 24:14-15

> *"Now fear the LORD and serve him with all faithfulness. Throw away the gods your forefathers worshiped beyond the River and in Egypt, and serve the LORD. But if serving the LORD seems undesirable to you, then choose for yourselves this day whom you will serve, whether the gods your forefathers served beyond the River, or the gods of the Amorites, in whose land you are living. But as for me and my household, we will serve the LORD."*

Father's Thoughts: Joshua answered the call. He and Caleb were the only two spies that had the guts to stand up and tell the Israelites that God would give them their promised land in spite of all obstacles. In this passage he has the guts to tell all the people straight out, 'I don't care about peer pressure or what anyone else is going to do. I am leading my family in the right direction, and I am answering God's call to serve him.'

Sons' Thoughts: A very simple ultimatum is given in this passage: Decide who you are going to follow, and devote yourself fully to whatever that may be. Don't let others, including parents and friends, tell you what to believe or do. You have to make that decision for yourself.

Discussion Questions: Do you have the guts to answer God's call in your life when others around you are not? Will you challenge me to do the same?

Notes: _____
_____
_____
_____

Thursday

Verse: Jonah 3:3

> *Jonah obeyed the word of the LORD and went to Nineveh. Now Nineveh was a very important city—a visit required three days.*

Father's Thoughts: When you get a chance, read the whole story of Jonah. Jonah was probably the most reluctant witness ever. He didn't like the people he was to witness to and it was a long trip. He decided at first to go in the opposite direction to get out of the trip. God forcefully (it really is funny, big fish and all) put him back in the right direction. In the end, he agreed, very reluctantly, to go ahead with the mission and lives were changed.

Sons' Thoughts: Jonah finally realized that hiding from God is an impossible task, and that God's will is always the best thing to do in all situations. (HWH)

Discussion Questions: Do you think that we can get out of doing God's work if we have a really bad attitude about it? Why do you think God continued to push Jonah and not just give up on him and send someone else?

Notes: _____
_____
_____
_____

Friday

Verse: Matthew 6:22-23

> *The eye is the lamp of the body. If your eyes are good, your whole body will be full of light. But if your eyes are bad, your whole body will be full of darkness. If then the light within you is darkness, how great is that darkness!*

Father's Thoughts: We have become a very visual society. Television, magazines, cable, movies, the Internet, all of these hold great opportunities for entertainment and for temptation. We really need to be wise about what we submit ourselves to and make sure that we do not throw fuel on a fire.

Sons' Thoughts: It's like a boat. Wherever the rudder goes, the whole ship is going to follow. This is why the eyes are so important. If we see something that is pleasing to the eye, we want to investigate more of what it is we see.

Discussion Questions: How can we as men regulate and manage this temptation? How do we gather the strength to just walk away, turn it off, put it down?

Notes: _____
_____
_____
_____

Week 41

B-Attitudes – Positive

There are times when I am just blown away by the logic and wisdom of Jesus. I shouldn't be. He IS God's son. The beatitudes are an example of the fantastic teaching Jesus gave at the "Sermon on the Mount". People from miles around had gathered to hear Him preach and he didn't disappoint them. The progression goes this way:

a) We must come to God recognizing our poor position in life, physically and spiritually.
b) We must come to God recognizing that we are hurt and are sinners – mourning life's challenges and our own shortcomings.
c) We must come to him with meekness and humility, acknowledging His power.
d) We should then begin to seek Him out, longing to be right with him through Jesus our Savior.
e) Once he is our Lord, we can begin to give of ourselves to others, being merciful and forgiving.
f) Then through His forgiveness we gain a purity that is visible in our relationship to Him
g) From that foundation we can begin to be leaders – peacemakers in this world.

Christ's followers, those closest to Him, were young men that GOT IT. They also knew they would have to face adversity. They knew that by following Christ, they would be tested, proven, and saved.

- B ready to come to Christ regardless of your circumstances.
- B ready to give it up to God and B humble.
- B ready to seek righteousness and then give it away.
- B ready to keep yourself clean and then help others do the same.
- B ready to take the good with the bad.

Challenge:
Men: Start to map out a plan for spiritual maturity with your young men. Help them understand their strengths and weaknesses.
Young Men: Look at the progression above, try to see where you are on the road to spiritual maturity. What are those attitudes that you need to work on the most.

B-Attitudes – Positive

Monday

Verse: Matthew 5:3-4

> *"Blessed are the poor in spirit, for theirs is the kingdom of heaven.*
> *Blessed are those who mourn, for they will be comforted.*

Father's Thoughts: We sometimes forget that half the battle to complete something great is getting past ourselves or past a situation we find ourselves in. God sees our current state, what we are lacking (poor in body, poor in spirit), or what is bugging us (whether we are down or sad) and he is willing to work with us in that state. By giving our issues to Him, we open ourselves up for His blessings regardless of the circumstances.

Sons' Thoughts: Those who go to Heaven are not those who believe they did it of their own accord. It is those who realize that they can't fight this battle alone, and who rely on the Savior to be our guiding hand throughout life.

Discussion Questions: What in your life do you find most discouraging? How do you take those things and give them to God?

Notes: _____
_____
_____
_____

Tuesday

Verse: Matthew 5:5

Blessed are the meek, for they will inherit the earth.

Father's Thoughts: Don't confuse meekness with weakness because they are not the same. Humility is a matter of knowing what you are good at and giving it up to the Lord for His glory and not your own. Meekness is controlling the strengths that God has given you. Self-controlled men are more likely to gain what they want than someone who is out of control and only looking at what they can gain out of life and from others.

Sons' Thoughts: Once again we find the characteristic of being humbled before God, knowing that we will fail without Him. But meekness is not one of shyness or timidity. It is doing something that is truly manly-admitting that you cannot do it alone, and that you need the Lord there to lift you up.

Discussion Questions: What do you believe is your greatest strength? Where have you been the most successful? Who got the glory for it, you, or God?

Notes: _____
_____
_____
_____

Wednesday

Verse: Matthew 5:6-7

> *Blessed are those who hunger and thirst for righteousness, for they will be filled.*
> *Blessed are the merciful, for they will be shown mercy.*

Father's Thoughts: The thirstiest that I have ever been was after an eight- hour hike from 6,000 feet up to 13,000 feet. I almost did not make it as I was suffering altitude sickness. A true friend, Greg Garrett, saw me struggling and helped me. He gave me some of his water and carried my backpack at a very critical time. I never knew thirst like I did that day; I never knew mercy like I did that day. Until the day, about a year later, that I gave my life to Christ. Now I am filled, now I know what mercy truly is. Thanks, Greg, for giving me an earthly example.

Sons' Thoughts: Matthew uses the concept of hunger and thirst here because he knows it is something we all can understand. We all know how it feels to truly be hungry or thirsty to the point where it hurts. We need to have this same longing for the righteousness that comes from God, and our lives will truly be sufficient.

Discussion Questions: Have you every wanted something so badly you would do anything to get it? Do you feel that way about doing the right thing all the time?

Notes: _____
_____
_____
_____

Thursday

Verse: Matthew 5:8-9

> *Blessed are the pure in heart, for they will see God.*
> *Blessed are the peacemakers, for they will be called sons of God.*

Father's Thoughts: I really like seeing these characteristics back –to- back as Jesus was teaching. I think it would be hard to be taken seriously as a leader, which is what a peacemaker really is, if you can't take the moral high ground. We have seen great leaders fall because they could not keep their sex drive in check. Get yourself right with God, and then others will look up to you with respect.

Sons' Thoughts: Being the peacemaker is a hard position, the only one speaking out to talk sense to both sides without becoming involved yourself can prove difficult. But we see the outcome of having this position of wisdom is one of true satisfaction from our Lord Jesus.

Discussion Questions: What sins do you struggle with the most? What is keeping you from being pure? (Remember, we are all guys here, it may hurt but let's be honest with each other). How can this keep you from fulfilling your dreams and ambitions?

Notes: _____
_____
_____
_____

Friday

Verse: Matthew 5:10-12

> *Blessed are those who are persecuted because of righteousness, for theirs is the kingdom of heaven.*
> *Blessed are you when people insult you, persecute you and falsely say all kinds of evil against you because of me. Rejoice and be glad, because great is your reward in heaven, for in the same way they persecuted the prophets who were before you.*

Father's Thoughts: Taking a stand for God has its risks. I know that I have been mocked; some don't even try to hide it. I have had bosses tell me that I am just too Christian. It is interesting that those same guys eventually came to me to discuss serious issues in their lives. I try not to get caught up in all the talk because this could bring me down. Instead, I try the best I can to bide my time and let God work. I am not always successful. I really don't like being talked down, but I am growing each day in my strength.

Sons' Thoughts: We usually do not mix having insults hurled at us with being glad and rejoicing. Also notice the wording here- not "if" people insult you, but "when". Living a Christian life will have its trying moments, but God encourages us to look past these at the big picture-pleasing the Lord with our faith.

Discussion Questions: Does anyone you know give you a hard time about your faith in Christ? Do you have Christian friends that are insulted? What is your reaction?

Notes: _____
_____
_____
_____

Week 42

B-Attitudes - Negative

One of the biggest mistakes that I have made so far has been going into a situation thinking I knew it all. I was going to be the best of the best of the best and I would do it in my sleep. That cockiness, rooted in immaturity, nearly cost me my job, and it did cost me a lot of respect.

Only after I calmed down and realized that I was in over my head did I begin to make progress. By the time I left, I had learned more from my mistakes and have been a better man for them. In the "Sermon on the Mount" Christ warned us about the problems that lay ahead, problems of our own making. How we learn from our mistakes will always mark our road to maturity, and repeating those mistakes could cost us dearly.

- B careful that you don't let success go to your head.
- B careful not to be self-serving.
- B careful to not fall for the charlatan.
- B careful not to judge- you have your own problems.
- B careful about what sprouts out.

Challenge:

Men: Help your young men to recognize symptoms that can lead to self-destruction. Discuss how they can work with you and with other Christian men to learn from their mistakes and mature in Christ.

Young Men: Recognize that life is full of risks and mistakes will happen. Listen to Christ's teaching and do your best to avoid major traps that can cause you to fall.

B-Attitudes - Negative

Monday

Verse: Luke 6:24-26

> *"But woe to you who are rich, for you have already received your comfort. Woe to you who are well fed now, for you will go hungry. Woe to you who laugh now, for you will mourn and weep. Woe to you when all men speak well of you, for that is how their fathers treated the false prophets.*

Father's Thoughts: Too much of a good thing can harm us. If we rely on our riches, if we become self-satisfied, if we make life one big game, we can be easily deceived. While we are encouraged to have strength in the tough times, we may need even more strength in the good times.

Sons' Thoughts: People who are content with being content with life as it is on earth without God are the ones that will be looking back on their lives, asking themselves, "Was all that I had satisfying?" and the answer will be no.HWH

Discussion Questions: When things are going well, do you sometimes forget to thank God, to acknowledge His hand in your success, forget to share those riches, that abundance with others who have needs?

Notes: _____
_____
_____
_____

Tuesday

Verse: Luke 6:32-34

> *"If you love those who love you, what credit is that to you? Even 'sinners' love those who love them. And if you do good to those who are good to you, what credit is that to you? Even 'sinners' do that. And if you lend to those from whom you expect repayment, what credit is that to you? Even 'sinners' lend to 'sinners,' expecting to be repaid in full.*

Father's Thoughts: What's in it for me? That is way too much of our modern culture. God knows the nature of the man he created, the weakness and selfishness. But He expects more. Once we come to Christ we should take on the image that He originally made us in, the one that is generous and self-sacrificing, the image that died for us.

Sons' Thoughts: Here's where we begin to separate ourselves from the world. Our society always gives to see what they will get in turn, and does things only for the benefit they will receive.

Discussion Questions: Where have you been generous to others? What is one opportunity you can take to help someone else? Write out a personal mission statement of things you can do to help others. Start at home.

Notes: _____
_____
_____

Wednesday

Verse: Luke 6:39

> *He also told them this parable: "Can a blind man lead a blind man? Will they not both fall into a pit?*

Father's Thoughts: We have a lot of people in this world that want things from you. There are more infomercials on TV than regular shows. There are people out there that want you to follow them, usually after you have paid them large sums of money, but follow them where? We should look at all those who tell us what we should do through Jesus- colored glasses. "What Would Jesus Do" is a catchy phrase…..and not a bad idea of how to filter the message and keep yourselves from following someone else who tells you he knows best.

Sons' Thoughts: Always be careful who you choose to model your behavior after and look up to in this world. While they may appear to have everything together, they are just as human as you are. Having a role model is not always a bad thing, just remember your beliefs and stay strong not to compromise them.

Discussion Questions: Do you consider yourselves a leader or a follower? Both, depending on the circumstances? Before you follow someone's lead, what questions should you ask them?

Notes: _____
_____
_____
_____

Thursday

Verse: Luke 6:41-42

> *"Why do you look at the speck of sawdust in your brother's eye and pay no attention to the plank in your own eye? How can you say to your brother, 'Brother, let me take the speck out of your eye,' when you yourself fail to see the plank in your own eye? You hypocrite, first take the plank out of your eye, and then you will see clearly to remove the speck from your brother's eye.*

Father's Thoughts: My college pastor had a great visual for this, a guy walks over to you and says, "Hey, you got something there in your eye, let me help you there...I will just lay this 2x4 on your shoulder while I get close enough to get it out." The fact is we all have flaws and self- help gurus make millions off people trying to overcome them. We should examine ourselves through Jesus' eyes, not those of others. We should examine others through Jesus' eyes and see what He sees, not what we claim to see.

Sons' Thoughts: We see those people all the time, who are overly quick to judge others. Why do you think they're like this? It's because they want to try and hide their own imperfections. Before we see something someone is doing wrong or struggling with, remember that we all have flaws, and try to help them with as open a mind as possible.

Discussion Questions: How can you help someone with their issues and flaws without coming off better than they are? What do you need to work on yourself?

Notes: _____
_____
_____
_____

Friday

Verse: Luke 6:43-45

> *"No good tree bears bad fruit, nor does a bad tree bear good fruit. Each tree is recognized by its own fruit. People do not pick figs from thornbushes, or grapes from briers. The good man brings good things out of the good stored up in his heart, and the evil man brings evil things out of the evil stored up in his heart. For out of the overflow of his heart his mouth speaks.*

Father's Thoughts: It's what's inside that counts, right? That is what Jesus is trying to get across to us. I must admit, I fall prey to being the happy, smiling Christian when what is brewing inside is far from righteous. Jesus dealt with it then and we deal with it now…people can have ulterior motives. I just pray that the closer I am in my relationship with Christ, the more he can change me, from the inside out.

Sons' Thoughts: We hear that a change must come from the inside out. And that's how we should truly go about things. Putting on some sort of appearance will not help our circumstances. If we truly want to feel a change, we must concentrate on fixing the inside first, and the outside will naturally follow suit.

Discussion Questions: Do you ever put on a false front? Do you know people that act one way in public and then another way in private? What do you need to change from the inside out?

Notes: _____
_____
_____
_____

Week 43

Self Confidence – Confidence in the Lord

—⁂—

When we were growing up in Taiwan we had to face the fiercest of storms, the Typhoon. Typhoons are the Pacific equivalent to a hurricane and are just as destructive. Because of where Taiwan is situated, two to four typhoons per year hit the island and cause major damage. For the first two years we would hunker down in our house, tape the windows to limit the shards of glass if a window broke, and then spent several hours mopping up the water that would always come in the house. During the first half of the storm we would work on one side of the house and then, after the eye of the storm passed, we would go to the other side and do the same.

After two years of fighting these storms, a losing battle at best, my brother had an idea. He designed wooden panels that would run along tracks above and below each window. When the storm came, we simply had to shut these over the windows and the storm water and wind would not hit them and we would be safe. It was a simple idea that worked to perfection. With the cover in place, we were safe in our house against the fierce storm. Unlike our neighbors, we could sleep peacefully. Jesus, through his sacrifice, has given us a confidence of eternal safety. The storms will come, but behind him we can be confident and rest in his love and peace.

Got to be content
- Comfortable in your own skin

Who is pointing the finger at you?
- It's not Him

Is the storm getting you wet?
- You are never alone.

Need some understanding?
- I'm rich, I'm rich?

Look down at the bottom
- What a great foundation

Challenge:

Men: Give your young men an understanding of where true confidence lies, in our relationship with God. Show them that the strongest men are those who build a firm foundation in Christ Jesus.

Young Men: Discuss what it means to feel good about yourself. Learn to build your confidence on God rather than basing it on other people or material things.

Self Confidence – Confidence in the Lord

Monday

Verse: 1 Timothy 6:9

But godliness with contentment is great gain.

Father's Thoughts: One of the biggest challenges youth are facing each day is what you do not have and who you are not. No matter who you are there will be others who have more than you, do things better than you, are better looking and smarter. It is easy as a teenager to let this get to you, especially if you have dreams and goals. What no one can take from you, what no one can do better than you, is your personal relationship to God. Yes, there will always be spiritual giants, but that is their relationship, not yours. So striving to be like him in your relationship with him, combined with satisfaction of who he made you, that is the godliness/contentment combo he wants to see.

Sons' Thoughts: Being content with yourself is a daunting challenge. We live in a society where we are constantly told that we should improve the way we look to fill a certain expectation. God made each one of us unique while being in His image. What greater gift can we receive than mirroring our creator?

Discussion Questions: What things are keeping you from being content with who you are? Discuss those things that make you most content and self confident.

Notes: _____
_____
_____

Tuesday

Verse: Romans 7:24 – 8:2

> *What a wretched man I am! Who will rescue me from this body of death? Thanks be to God—through Jesus Christ our Lord!*
> *So then, I myself in my mind am a slave to God's law, but in the sinful nature a slave to the law of sin. Therefore, there is now no condemnation for those who are in Christ Jesus, because through Christ Jesus the law of the Spirit of life set me free from the law of sin and death.*

Father's Thoughts: If Jesus is not condemning us, why then do we beat ourselves up? Sometimes I know that when I have fallen short of God's law, I take it hard. Then I step back and realize that the reason I take it hard is that I really want to do what is right and that is a step in the right direction. Jesus is not a spiritual policeman setting a speed trap; he is simply encouraging us to do the right thing.

Sons' Thoughts: No one can serve two masters. Here in this verse, Paul explains how in our minds we are held captive by our sinful nature, but God comes and frees us of these chains. We constantly beat ourselves up because we make mistakes; after all, we are only human. But keep in mind, these mistakes are not what define you. The Lord overcame any mistake we made or will make the day he was nailed to the cross and died the death of humanity.

Discussion Questions: Where in your life do you tend to 'beat yourself up?' What can you do to help you gain confidence that you are moving in the right direction?

Notes: _____
_____
_____
_____

Wednesday

Verse: Psalm 46:1-7

> *God is our refuge and strength, an ever-present help in trouble.*
> *Therefore we will not fear, though the earth give way and the mountains fall into the heart of the sea,*
> *Though its waters roar and foam and the mountains quake with their surging.*
> *Selah*
> *There is a river whose streams make glad the city of God, the holy place where the Most High dwells.*
> *God is within her, she will not fall; God will help her at break of day.*
> *Nations are in uproar, kingdoms fall; he lifts his voice, the earth melts.*
> *The LORD Almighty is with us; the God of Jacob is our fortress.*
> *Selah*

Father's Thoughts: This Psalm from the Sons of Korah (temple assistants) is a reminder that God is always there to help us when we feel all alone. The situation you are in might seem tough, even hopeless, but in the midst of all the pain and uncertainty He is with you. As teenagers, you may be going through things for the first time, and while it may seem awful for the moment, each trial is a learning tool. By learning to be confident in God now, you are maturing for all of the battles you will face in life.

Sons' Thoughts: A few months ago, I was asked to stand up in front of the entire church congregation and read this exact passage, something I was quite nervous about. But as I was reading the words, they immediately comforted me. These verses show the true power of God, and provide us with words of encouragement when we feel the fear begin to creep into our thoughts. My challenge is to memorize this passage and keep it in the storage box of your mind for those days you must turn to the Lord for encouragement.

Discussion Questions: What is the toughest challenge you face on a day –to- day basis? What do you think God can teach you by guiding you through this time? Do you truly believe He is wise and knowledgeable enough to guide you through?

Notes: _____

_____
_____
_____

Thursday

Verse: Colossians 2:1-3

> *I want you to know how much I am struggling for you and for those at Laodicea, and for all who have not met me personally. My purpose is that they may be encouraged in heart and united in love, so that they may have the full riches of complete understanding, in order that they may know the mystery of God, namely, Christ, in whom are hidden all the treasures of wisdom and knowledge.*

Father's Thoughts: Part of being confident is knowing in what or whom you can put your confidence. When I was in 2nd grade I had a friend that was one of the nicest guys, but he was huge. Not fat huge, just really, really big. It was easy to feel good when you were around him because you felt safe. God is bigger, stronger and wiser than anyone we can hang with on earth. Through Christ we can have extreme confidence.

Sons' Thoughts: There must always be understanding for there to be confidence. To be confident in something, we must know every aspect of it, to make sure it won't turn out a completely different way than we expect. We can always have confidence in God. As we grow in our Christian walk, it will be easier and easier to understand God's plan for our life, providing us with the confidence we need to face whatever struggles may block our path.

Discussion Questions: When have you been the most confident in your abilities? What made you gain that confidence - skill, practice, coaching or teaching? How can you learn to gain more confidence in spiritual things?

Notes: _____
_____
_____
_____

Friday

Verse: Hebrews 3:3-6

> *Jesus has been found worthy of greater honor than Moses, just as the builder of a house has greater honor than the house itself. For every house is built by someone, but God is the builder of everything. Moses was faithful as a servant in all God's house, testifying to what would be said in the future. But Christ is faithful as a son over God's house. And we are his house, if we hold on to our courage and the hope of which we boast.*

Father's Thoughts: Through our relationship with Jesus Christ, we can gain courage for whatever comes against us. Using the picture of a house, Christ is shown as the leader of that house and in this house, we are safe. In our life with Christ we can be confident in the walls, the roof and the foundation that God has built.

Sons' Thoughts: This verse explains how we are houses of God. The most vital part of the house is its foundation, without it the whole things crumbles. The courage and hope mentioned at the end of the verse are the foundation of which I speak. With these characteristics we slowly construct our ministry, finally building a haven for those who are lost to seek out the Lord Jesus.

Discussion Questions: Have there been times in your life that you feel unsafe and afraid? What helped you to get past those times? How does your faith in Christ give you a foundation for getting through the tough times?

Notes: _____
_____
_____
_____

Week 44

God's Mighty Athletes

I tried my hand at several sports when I was young, including church basketball, little league baseball, rugby and soccer. In high school, growing up in Asia, we did not have all the traditional high school sports but we did have intramural baseball and football. I was mildly successful in baseball as my long lanky frame was suited for 1st base. That same frame meant football did not last long. However, as an adult I fell in love with racquetball. It had all the elements that I wanted- aerobic exercise, fast competition, the ability to hit your opponent in the back of the head with a non-lethal projectile.

Six years ago as I was playing with my friend Ken Luke, I went for a smash overhead shot. It was not one I would normally hit but we were just goofing around so I hit it anyway. Immediately following the shot, my arm fell to my side, useless, while the pain I felt was nothing I had ever known before. Surgery three months later repaired the torn labrum but nothing I can do mentally has been able to get me back on the court. I just can't do it. Needless to say, I am not the world's greatest athlete. I have enjoyed the fact that all three of my kids enjoy and have had success in sports. God knows that most men love sports and competition and he has wired us that way. It is something for men to enjoy together, for sons and fathers to share, and in his Word he helps to illustrate life through the eyes of aathlete.

Playing by the rules
- Win fair and square

Feel like a champ
- Celebrate with the sunrise.

The King of endurance
- He never wears out.

I may be old but…..
- Even you young kids get gassed

Better than an energy drink
- Putting our hope in God

Challenge:

Men: Whether it is sports or some other activity, use physical involvement with your young man to teach him lessons of love, life, loyalty to our loving God who gave us bodies that move.

Young Men: Whether you are an athlete, a weekend warrior or not, take heart in the bodies you were given and take care of them. Use the energy and strength God gave you to interact with others and to learn from your body God's great gift of life and health.

God's Mighty Athletes

Monday

Verse: 2 Timothy 2:5

Similarly, if anyone competes as an athlete, he does not receive the victor's crown unless he competes according to the rules.

Father's Thoughts: By the time you are a senior in high school you will have seen enough athletic events to know there are those who will do anything to win. Whether it is breaking a small rule here or there or going to the extreme with steroids or other drugs, cheating is cheating and the consequences will be disqualification if caught, or a guilty conscience or worse, bodily harm. Paul loved to compare the Christian walk with athletics; maybe he had been an athlete or a coach. He knew the importance of running a fair race, competing within the rules, doing the right thing.

Sons' Thoughts: This passage talks about performing in some sort of athletic competition. Many times during some kind of competition we face the temptation of cheating. Paul encourages Timothy against this and tells him he will be rewarded far more greatly for not giving in.

Discussion Questions: As you approach life in Christ, are you willing to stay within the rules? How do you know what these are? Are there any temptations you have faced recently in your life's race? How did you deal with them?

Notes: _____
_____
_____
_____

Tuesday

Verse: Psalm 19:1-5

> *The heavens declare the glory of God;*
> *the skies proclaim the work of his hands.*
> *Day after day they pour forth speech;*
> *night after night they display knowledge.*
> *There is no speech or language*
> *where their voice is not heard.*
> *Their voice goes out into all the earth,*
> *their words to the ends of the world.*
> *In the heavens he has pitched a tent for the sun,*
> *which is like a bridegroom coming forth from his pavilion,*
> *like a champion rejoicing to run his course.*

Father's Thoughts: It is an old movie but I love the scene in *Rocky* where at the end of a long run he stands on the steps overlooking Philadelphia and he raises his arms in triumph. I can also remember my wedding day, how proud I felt when my bride walked towards me as I stood waiting at the altar. In the same way, the very nature that God created displays pride in reflecting His magnificence. Shouldn't we?

Sons' Thoughts: Nature practically screams the wonders of God and his creation. To me, everything just seems to work in such perfect harmony to be an accident. God had a plan in mind when he created each one of us. And athletic or not, we each have gifts we can offer to the kingdom of heaven.

Discussion Questions: What is the most beautiful place you have been to in your life? What does that place tell you about God? What has been your greatest achievement? Did you remember to praise God for how He made you?

Notes: _____
_____
_____
_____

Wednesday

Verse: Isaiah 40:28-29

Do you not know?
Have you not heard?
The LORD is the everlasting God,
the Creator of the ends of the earth.
He will not grow tired or weary,
and his understanding no one can fathom.
He gives strength to the weary
and increases the power of the weak.

Father's Thoughts: I love to watch my son wrestle. In the third period, when he is gassed, I hope that he remembers this verse and perseveres. We can have confidence that in our spiritual struggles, when we think we cannot go another step, He gives us strength and power.

Sons' Thoughts: If running and working out were easy to do, then everyone would be doing it. But the only way to get better at something is to push yourself to the limit. But growing tired and weary is an earthly attribute. But God, serving as our spiritual energy boost, never stops to rest, providing us with the strength we need to persevere.

Discussion Questions: In what situations have you felt exhausted both physically and spiritually? Have you called on Christ for strength; do you believe he will provide it?

Notes: _____
_____
_____
_____

Thursday

Verse: Isaiah 40:30

*Even youths grow tired and weary,
and young men stumble and fall;*

Father's Thoughts: This is great to know. As an old guy, I thought I was the only one that got really tired and worn out. God knows we can all get down but I thank Him daily that he lifts us up and gives us encouragement. We need to learn young that we will have days that will be tough, but we are all in the boat together. Through Christ we can gain strength. Through the fellowship of believers we can bounce back.

Sons' Thoughts: There you go, a verse talking directly to us young'uns. Contrary to popular belief, the bible is not just for those over the age of 30. Everyone has days where they feel physically and spiritually drained. But God will always be there, whether we are 16 or 60.

Discussion Questions: What are the things that you do that make you the most tired physically? Do you get tired spiritually? How does God "wake us up"?

Notes: _____
_____
_____
_____

Friday

Verse: Isaiah 40:31

> *but those who hope in the LORD*
> *will renew their strength.*
> *They will soar on wings like eagles;*
> *they will run and not grow weary,*
> *they will walk and not be faint.*

Father's Thoughts: I had to stop running over the last few months due to problems with my left hip. It has been really disappointing because I had grown to love it. I thank God that through Christ I will never have to put away my spiritual running, my spiritual exercise. That is why relying on the Lord for all things is so important, worship is so vital. Without these exercises we would soon experience atrophy of the heart.

Sons' Thoughts: As young men, we might take our ability to run and exercise for granted. It's not something we will always be able to do on our time here on earth. But we will always have the opportunity to be spiritually fit; now we only have to take advantage of that wonderful gift by exercising regularly our spiritual body.

Discussion Questions: What activities do you love the most and how would you feel if you had to give them up? What spiritual activities do you think God is calling you to do? What would happen if you choose not to do these 'exercises'?

Notes: _____
_____
_____
_____

Week 45

Is this for Real?

—⚞—

Every generation of believers faces new and equally tough challenges to their faith. In facing these constant challenges we must be careful that we do not water down our faith just to be seen as "tolerant." My generation was bombarded with science, as if that in some way explained away God. But the deeper you dive into science, the more real God becomes. You begin to see into His creativity and his enjoyment, even his sense of humor.

This generation faces 'spirituality,' warm and fuzzy feel-good with no substance, and the 'new-age' view. It doesn't matter what you believe, just as long as you believe something and feel good about it. Hey, I feel really good about my Labrador but I haven't built a cult around her. I hope we have a faith that is stronger than someone who applies to be ordained as a minister over the internet at lunch time. We need to train each other up to give an account for our faith with a strong, dignified, gentle and honest defense of our faith in Christ, the risen Lord.

Hear that Big Bang?
- It was God calling it into order.

So you won't listen to this guy
- How about my kid?

This is the way
- Can I be any clearer?

Did anyone tell you guys to run that way?
- Running to instead of from

This is a test.
- Have you studied?

Challenge:

Men: Your young man's faith will be tested every day. Work with him to give him confidence in the reality of his faith and the truth of his walk with Christ.

Young Men: Arm yourselves with the confidence that God is real and Jesus Christ is our savior. Be ready to give an account for your faith when challenged.

Is this for Real?

Monday

Verse: Colossians 1:15-20

> *He is the image of the invisible God, the firstborn over all creation. For by him all things were created: things in heaven and on earth, visible and invisible, whether thrones or powers or rulers or authorities; all things were created by him and for him. He is before all things, and in him all things hold together. And he is the head of the body, the church; he is the beginning and the firstborn from among the dead, so that in everything he might have the supremacy. For God was pleased to have all his fullness dwell in him, and through him to reconcile to himself all things, whether things on earth or things in heaven, by making peace through his blood, shed on the cross.*

Father's Thoughts: When I had an opportunity in college to witness to a young Japanese man about Christ, I found that I had to be much more basic. I had to convince him first that there even was a God. The Trinity, a three-fold understanding of the Father, Son and Holy Spirit is a difficult teaching and one I will leave to theologians. What I know is: God is real and through Jesus Christ He is revealed to man. Nature reveals Him and our hearts' relationship with him reveals Him to us. Jesus is Lord.

Sons' Thoughts: Sorry, Big Bang Theory, you're not gonna cut it. I have to believe we were created by something with the ability to love and have a plan. God's plan was for the world to be saved by whom he held most dear to Him, his one and only son. I know God is real when I look around and see his plans moving into action.

Discussion Questions: When do you feel God is most real to you? Why do you think that God chooses to reveal himself through His Son?

Notes:

Tuesday

Verse: Hebrews 1:1-4

> *In the past God spoke to our forefathers through the prophets at many times and in various ways, but in these last days he has spoken to us by his Son, whom he appointed heir of all things, and through whom he made the universe. The Son is the radiance of God's glory and the exact representation of his being, sustaining all things by his powerful word. After he had provided purification for sins, he sat down at the right hand of the Majesty in heaven. So he became as much superior to the angels as the name he has inherited is superior to theirs.*

Father's Thoughts: I look in the mirror and I see my dad. Well, I have my mom's nose and other characteristics, but I am my dad in so many ways. You look young now, guys, but when you get older, you too will look like your parents. In that same way Jesus reflected His Father. He gave us a sampling of God, His wisdom, kindness and love. We know God when we know His Son.

Sons' Thoughts: God realized that when he spoke through the prophets in the olden times, there was still that human barrier that sometimes hindered His will from completely taking effect. So what better way to speak to His people than by sending someone who shares His very being, someone who knows the thoughts of the Father?

Discussion Questions: What is the best trait that you have received from your parents? Do people see the best of your parents in you? How can we reflect the best of Jesus within us to the world around us?

Notes: _____
_____
_____
_____

Wednesday

Verse: John 14:6-7

> *Jesus answered, "I am the way and the truth and the life. No one comes to the Father except through me. If you really knew me, you would know my Father as well. From now on, you do know him and have seen him."*

Father's Thoughts: There are people that do not believe in our Savior who will say, "He was a good man and a great prophet." What they are really saying is, "He isn't who he says he is." One of the best lines in *Remember the Titans* was "Leave no doubt." Jesus was extremely clear; he is the ONLY way, not one of many, to be reconciled with God.

Sons' Thoughts: Our faith is separated from others because we believe in a God who actually claimed to be the Savior of the world, and this may be one of the big reasons why people do not believe. They don't like the thought of only having one way to do things. But Jesus states it clearly- the one and only way to reach the Father in heaven is through Him and Him alone.

Discussion Questions: Why do you think that people seek to find so many ways to get to God outside of Christ? Discuss together how you can make the point clear in your own lives and in your dealings with others that Christ is the Way.

Notes: _____
_____
_____
_____

Thursday

Verse: Acts 4:13-15

> *When they saw the courage of Peter and John and realized that they were unschooled, ordinary men, they were astonished and they took note that these men had been with Jesus. But since they could see the man who had been healed standing there with them, there was nothing they could say. So they ordered them to withdraw from the Sanhedrin and then conferred together.*

Father's Thoughts: One of the clearest signals to me of Christ's reality is in the actions of the men that followed Him. His closest confidants, His friends, His disciples had the greatest insight into His life and to who he was. They personally witnessed His death. Were he a fraud, were He not real, I do not believe you would have seen the strength and courage of His followers. They knew, Christ is Risen!

Sons' Thoughts: After the disciples witnessed Jesus alive again after suffering a brutal death, we immediately see a change in their lives. Nothing else in this world could influence someone to face such horrible persecution and death (Bartholomew was skinned alive) than the belief of a truly risen Savior.

Discussion Questions: What makes Christ real to you? Knowing the risen Savior, are you willing to go out and boldly tell people about Him? What is holding you back?

Notes: _____
_____
_____
_____

Friday

Verse: 1 Peter 3:15

But in your hearts set apart Christ as Lord. Always be prepared to give an answer to everyone who asks you to give the reason for the hope that you have. But do this with gentleness and respect,

Father's Thoughts: The best way to be prepared for a test is to have studied it enough to be confident in the material. It's the same in being bold for Christ and the challenges you will face when you take a stand for Him. We have to study the scriptures, spend time in prayer and worship, so we can be ready.

Sons' Thoughts: It's a given. If you live your life in a Christ-like manner, people will notice and ask questions. We must pray for the strength to embrace these situations and prepare ourselves to share the reason for our faith.

Discussion Questions: Are you confident in your knowledge of God and His son Jesus? What can you do to be more prepared to give an accounting of what you believe? Who do you know that might try and challenge you?

Notes: _____
_____
_____
_____

Week 46

Death Comes Knocking

No man should bury his children. I am blessed with three that are extremely healthy but life is fragile and disease and accidents are part of life. When our daughter had to undergo emergency surgery a couple of years ago the pain and fear of possible loss was staring us in the face. Within the last year two prominent Christian men, Stephen Curtis Chapman and Rick Burgess, lost children to accidents. Both showed me the power of God's love overcoming loss. If you want to know how a real man handles grief, go to www.rickandbubba.com and watch the video of Rick celebrating the life of his son.

God knows the pain of losing a son, His only Son, and we are saved by that act of pain and sacrifice. We cannot sugarcoat death here on earth, we can only conquer it. Eternal life is a hard concept for teenagers and for adults, but it is God's free gift through Jesus. As men, society has tried to shape the way we grieve, shape the way we think about the end of life. But for those who know our savior Jesus Christ, death holds a whole different context- we are going home. Each person who reads this will have had a different level of experience with death. Some may have lost a family member or two, some may have lost many. Others may have dealt with cancer or with another horrible disease. The end game is still the same, God has that covered. We can be confident in him to both take us through the tough times and then shatter death at the end of the day.

Death has been conquered.
- We can come along with Him.

It is a dark and forbidding valley road.
- But we are not alone.

There is a new Sheriff in town.
- A new order to things around here

You won't get this kid until you pry my....
- No, you will never get him.

Hey, you! Yeah you, Mr. Death!
- You ain't got nothin on me now.

Challenge:

Men: Share with your young man your own experience with death and sorrow. Teach him to handle the pain and grief through the eyes of God and through the confidence they have in Jesus Christ.

Young Men: Share your thoughts and possible fear of death. Talk about how you might react to the death of someone you love. Talk about how God can guide you through it.

Death Comes Knocking

Monday

Verse: 1 Thessalonians 4:13-14

> *Brothers, we do not want you to be ignorant about those who fall asleep, or to grieve like the rest of men, who have no hope. We believe that Jesus died and rose again and so we believe that God will bring with Jesus those who have fallen asleep in him.*

Father's Thoughts: Christians really should have a very different view of death than non-Christians. When a fellow Christian dies, whether a family member or friend, the grief is real. But with the hope we have in Christ we should look back on their lives with joy and the hope that eternal life brings.

Sons' Thoughts: The world's view on death is one of an end; however, as Christians we should view death as a beginning, the beginning to a never-ending time of worship with our Father in Heaven. I love singing. I am at one of my happiest moments singing praises to God. When I think about doing this for eternity once I am in Heaven, I no longer think of death as a terrible ordeal.

Discussion Questions: Have you had to deal with the death of someone you love? How does your faith allow you to approach death with hope? Can that hope outweigh the sorrow?

Notes: _____
_____
_____
_____

Tuesday

Verse: Psalm 23:4

> *Even though I walk through the valley of the shadow of death,*
> *I will fear no evil, for you are with me; your rod and your staff,*
>   *they comfort me.*

Father's Thoughts: This is a tough one because I know friends who have lost a child. As a deacon, I visit people in the hospital that are facing true life -and -death situations. With God's help, and the trust we have in Christ, we can face those times knowing that the God of eternity is always with us no matter how hard the road.

Sons' Thoughts: As boys maturing into adulthood, we are not as familiar with death as we will be when we begin to age. If we face the death of a loved one around us, it has the potential to throw our mind into turmoil. But always keep in mind that God has a master plan for the world, and that person whose time came was not overlooked by God, but used by God to fulfill his purpose for the universe.

Discussion Questions: What is your greatest fear? How can you give that over to Jesus and know that He walks with us through any and every tough battle?

Notes: _____
_____
_____
_____

Wednesday

Verse: Revelation 21:4

> *He will wipe every tear from their eyes. There will be no more death or mourning or crying or pain, for the old order of things has passed away."*

Father's Thoughts: As Christians our hope should not be short-sighted. We need to gain comfort in the eventual second coming of Christ. Eternal life in Christ is just that, eternal, so earthly or bodily death is only a consequence of our sin against God and His perfect ways, not an end to our relationship with Him.

Sons' Thoughts: This is another reason why death should also be celebrated. When a Christian dies and goes to Heaven, he will know nothing of earthly pain. He will not even remember any suffering he experienced in his time on earth. The only feeling in his being will be one of praise to his heavenly Father.

Discussion Questions: What is the most pain you have ever endured physically? How did you manage to get past it? Are you convinced that God has control of all physical and spiritual pain?

Notes: _____
_____
_____
_____

Thursday

Verse: Romans 8:37-39

> *No, in all these things we are more than conquerors through him who loved us. For I am convinced that neither death nor life, neither angels nor demons, neither the present nor the future, nor any powers, neither height nor depth, nor anything else in all creation, will be able to separate us from the love of God that is in Christ Jesus our Lord.*

Father's Thoughts: Have you heard stories of unfortunate people that get in between a large animal and their young? The bear, the moose, the buffalo, and the cougar will all attack and possibly kill anyone that stands between them and the child they love and nurture. Even these examples don't give justice to the ferociousness with which God protects His children. God is God and he is the Father of our souls when we accept His salvation through Jesus Christ. When death knocks, we know who will answer the door.

Sons' Thoughts: This reminds me of the old footsteps poem that my grandmother has had taped to her refrigerator since I can remember. A man looks back on his life as if they were footsteps on a beach. He sees two sets except for when he was going through really tough times. He looks at Jesus and asks him why this is. Jesus looks at him and says, "It was in these tough times that I carried you." To me, that is the perfect picture of God's love for us.

Discussion Questions: Do you recognize that you are under His protection? What is a time that you have been most afraid? How did you get through it?

Notes: _____
_____
_____
_____

Friday

Verse: 1 Corinthians 15:51-55

> *Listen, I tell you a mystery: We will not all sleep, but we will all be changed— in a flash, in the twinkling of an eye, at the last trumpet. For the trumpet will sound, the dead will be raised imperishable, and we will be changed. For the perishable must clothe itself with the imperishable, and the mortal with immortality. When the perishable has been clothed with the imperishable, and the mortal with immortality, then the saying that is written will come true:*
>
> *"Death has been swallowed up in victory."*
> *Where, O death, is your victory?*
> *Where, O death, is your sting?"*

Father's Thoughts: When you win a wrestling match, finish first in a race, have the highest score on a test, or win the heart of the girl, the victory is sweet. These victories are short-lived because you will have to turn around and do it all over again (well, maybe not win the girl's heart – 23 years of wonderful marriage and counting). Christ's victory over death is final, complete, done. So much so that Paul felt like mocking it. Our God has re-written the ending of the lives of all who accept salvation through Jesus Christ.

Sons' Thoughts: It sounds as if Paul is trash talking death here at the end of this verse. But this is the approach we should take against death. Jesus, while on the cross, has already conquered death for us, providing us with immortality- not on earth where we face hurt and defeat, but in Heaven where we can feel no pain or sorrow.

Discussion Questions: What is the greatest thing you have ever accomplished? Did it take a lot of hard work and sacrifice? How did Jesus sacrifice to conquer death?

Notes:

Week 47

Hope for Something Better

—⟨⟨⟨—

A dear friend of mine and fellow deacon at my church is Carl Wayne Meekins. Carl Wayne is a country singer (gee, go figure, we live in Nashville), song writer and painter who has inspired many men in our church with his life's story. Carl Wayne grew up with an alcoholic father who at various times abused and abandoned the family. He was a man motivated by material things and his favorite saying was, "I want to see life through a Cadillac window." Carl Wayne's song "Cadillac Window" says this:

> He wanted everybody to see him through a Cadillac window,
> "Hey, everybody, look at me!"
> Didn't know what he would have to sacrifice to pay that high price,
> Just to show his buddies he could succeed.
> Thought he could hide the lies in the car he drives
> He was broke and a drunk and everybody knew.
> Saw his family leave him through a Cadillac window,
> Said: "let 'em walk, they just get in my way"
> But I can see right through your Cadillac window.
> Yeah, I saw that man today through a Cadillac window,
> He passed right by me, nothing to say, I stood and cried and waved goodbye,
> As I watched that hearse carry my dad to his grave.

While his dad only put his hope in material things, Carl Wayne has put his trust in Christ and through Him has hope that his dad never knew and has become the dad that his father never could be.

- Hope – through confidence in Christ's authority
- Hope – through a God that created all things
- Hope – through a Savior that deeply, deeply loves us
- Hope – through a Savior that conquered death
- Hope – through His Spirit that fills us with joy and peace

Challenge:

Men: We are constantly bombarded with bad news. Work to move your son beyond that quagmire and into the hope that is offered us through Jesus Christ

Young Men: Don't let 'em get you down. We are all facing challenges in this world, competing interests for our allegiance. Work together to face these challenges with Christ and fellow believers and don't put your hope in anything less.

Hope for Something Better

Monday

Verse: Luke 7:6-10

So Jesus went with them.
He was not far from the house when the centurion sent friends to say to him: "Lord, don't trouble yourself, for I do not deserve to have you come under my roof. That is why I did not even consider myself worthy to come to you. But say the word, and my servant will be healed. For I myself am a man under authority, with soldiers under me. I tell this one, 'Go,' and he goes; and that one, 'Come,' and he comes. I say to my servant, 'Do this,' and he does it."
When Jesus heard this, he was amazed at him, and turning to the crowd following him, he said, "I tell you, I have not found such great faith even in Israel." Then the men who had been sent returned to the house and found the servant well.

Father's Thoughts: I have to echo what Jesus said. Wow, here is a guy who is very unlikely to believe in Jesus, yet he understood the source of the power. This is the level of confidence that we need when we have to deal with something challenging. We hope for the best, not based on our own cleverness, but because we know who is in charge.

Sons' Thoughts: The man in this story had complete confidence in the power of Jesus. So much so that he did not even consider his house a place worthy enough to shelter the Son of God. He had the hope that Jesus could do anything and everything. And because of that hope, the Lord blessed him with his request.

Discussion Questions: How seriously do you take the power that Christ has on earth and heaven? What doubt do you have and how can you begin to eliminate those doubts?

Notes:

Tuesday

Verse: Romans 8:15-19

> *For you did not receive a spirit that makes you a slave again to fear, but you received the Spirit of sonship. And by him we cry, "Abba, Father." The Spirit himself testifies with our spirit that we are God's children. Now if we are children, then we are heirs—heirs of God and co-heirs with Christ, if indeed we share in his sufferings in order that we may also share in his glory.*

Father's Thoughts: I really love my dad. It does not mean that we always got along all the time because I was not always the best kid. Even today I have confidence in his advice and strength. Being his son really means a lot. Being God's son, being called worthy to be His son, means a lot, too. It means we share everything, good and bad. It means everything we have is His, and vice-versa. It's a family thing.

Sons' Thoughts: We are constantly plagued with that question, "what does your dad do for a living"? We are judged based upon who our Fathers are, what they have accomplished. So how wonderful is it to say, My Father created the universe, created me in His own image, and died so that I may have life!

Discussion Questions: Why do you thing that God wants us to call Him "Abba", the equivalent of "Daddy"? When are you closest to your earthly father? When do feel closest to God?

Notes: _____
_____
_____
_____

Wednesday

Verse: Luke 19:41-42

> *As he approached Jerusalem and saw the city, he wept over it and said" If you, even you, had only known this day what would bring you peace—but now it is hidden from your eyes."*

Father's Thoughts: It is rare to see men cry. We often build a hard shell around ourselves and keep our deepest emotions hidden. Maybe we think it is a sign of weakness or we feel it is feminine, or we simply do not think it is what a man would do. Yet Jesus, being a strong example of a man, wept. He did reserve his tears for his deepest emotions – the death of a close friend and what he saw as the eternal death of many people who would not accept God's plan. Jesus had a hope for Jerusalem, a hope that they would choose Him, and live.

Sons' Thoughts: Jesus looks at the main city in Jerusalem and realizes how corrupt they have become. He loves them so much that he weeps out loud because he knows what they are doing to themselves. Jesus shows how passionately he feels towards those who do not believe in Him, and now He has trusted us with the job of reaching out to those very same people.

Discussion Questions: What are the things in your life you feel most passionate about, to the point of your deepest emotions? Do you have a heart for the lost so strong that it can bring you to tears? Are you willing to share with them the hope of Jesus?

Notes: _____
_____
_____

Thursday

Verse: 1 Timothy 4:9-10

> *This is a trustworthy saying that deserves full acceptance (and for this we labor and strive), that we have put our hope in the living God, who is the Savior of all men, and especially of those who believe.*

Father's Thoughts: As Christians in a modern world we get accused of all sorts of bad things. The one I hear a lot lately is that we are elitist and exclusionary. If we as the Church have become that, we should be ashamed, we are in the wrong. We must understand that Christ is the hope of ALL. We should, of all people, be an example of love and acceptance. Not accepting sin, but loving and accepting the sinner.

Sons' Thoughts: When I got into a conversation with a guy on my wrestling team about church, he claimed that it was a place for the narrow-minded. And while, yes, we do believe there is one God and one way to Heaven, it is not reserved for only one group of people. Jesus made the way to Heaven open to all who truly accept it, no matter the circumstances.

Discussion Questions: How can you reach out to those that may not have a great impression of the church? What barriers do we need to break down that might be keeping some away from Christ?

Notes: _____
_____
_____
_____

Friday

Verse: Romans 15:13

> *May the God of hope fill you with all joy and peace as you trust in him, so that you may overflow with hope by the power of the Holy Spirit.*

Father's Thoughts: There really is only one way to be full of hope and that is to be filled with the Holy Spirit and accept the hope that comes through salvation. I personally have a problem with trust. Like many men I am an A-type personality and think I can do everything by myself. I imagine you are the same way about many things. I hope that I can give up that selfishness and learn to fully rely on God.

Sons' Thoughts: The hope of those who have Christ on their side is like that of no other. They know that with Christ all things are possible, and are not held back by the limitations of this world. I am a person who likes to do things on my own, independent of others. But without God, my strivings will be futile.

Discussion Questions: What parts of your life are you holding back and not fully giving to God? How might that affect your relationship with Him?

Notes: _____
_____
_____
_____

Week 48

Being Prepared – Because You Never Know

—⚋—

I look back on my life and I see some pretty crazy and amazing things. To date, I have moved or relocated twenty-one times. Most of those occurred as a kid and when I was single, but a number have happened with the family, a consequence of corporate life. Yet, every step, every misstep seems to have prepared me for the next great adventure. God has both a sense of humor and a plan. I grew up in Southeast Asia, and later I found myself working in China due largely to that experience. There I had opportunities to grow, to witness and to build for the future. Add to that a lifetime of international business that has prepared me for international mission opportunities and leadership. I have had the chance to work with Chinese Bible study classes and see lives changed, all because of my background. When I was in 9th grade I took an education class and ended up tutoring special needs kids. The young boy I tutored was severely handicapped and had been abandoned by his family. He was then living with his aunt and uncle. It was the most tiring and challenging experience I have ever had. Yet, 35 years later on a mission trip to Hong Kong, I was prepared mentally and spiritually to work with an autistic child during a vacation Bible school.

God is working in our lives. We may not always see it and the process may seem to be painful but he is working in us and through us if we are willing to give ourselves to Him. That is why through prayer, study and fellowship, we should stand ready to take on the next great challenge for the Kingdom of God.

You have to be prepared to:

- Listen to God even when what you hear is not popular to others.
- Endure life's curveballs, they may come at you fast and low.
- Take a stand and resist temptations that come your way.
- Lead when presented the opportunity.
- Forgive the past and praise God for the path.

Challenge:

Men: Map out your life and spiritual journey. Share with your young man the key things in your life that have shaped you and prepared you to do God's work.

Young Men: Share with your father the things in life that are shaping you. Even though you are young, discuss those situations, activities and experiences that have already begun to shape and teach you.

Being Prepared – Because You Never Know

Monday

Verse: Genesis 37:5-8

> *Joseph had a dream, and when he told it to his brothers, they hated him all the more. He said to them, "Listen to this dream I had: We were binding sheaves of grain out in the field when suddenly my sheaf rose and stood upright, while your sheaves gathered around mine and bowed down to it." His brothers said to him, "Do you intend to reign over us? Will you actually rule us?" And they hated him all the more because of his dream and what he had said.*

Father's Thoughts: Be prepared – God might speak to you and send you in a direction that will not be popular with others. Joseph was a young kid with not much political savvy. One thing he did have was an ability to dream. Under God's leadership he would go on to do great things. It does not mean that everyone will be able to dream the same dream or share your vision.

Sons' Thoughts: Joseph found his purpose in life at a young age. He was to become a great leader to do God's will. And while this was not what his brothers wanted to hear, he did not shy away from what God wanted him to accomplish. When our plans in life do not always receive the reactions we want from those around us, do not let it stop you. God has you moving in this direction for a reason, and no earthly circumstances will be able to stop it from going the way He planned.

Discussion Questions: Have you examined your life to see areas that God may be leading you in? What do you think is your purpose in life, a purpose that only you can fulfill?

Notes:

Tuesday

Verse: Genesis 37:26-28

> *Judah said to his brothers, "What will we gain if we kill our brother and cover up his blood? Come, let's sell him to the Ishmaelites and not lay our hands on him; after all, he is our brother, our own flesh and blood." His brothers agreed. So when the Midianite merchants came by, his brothers pulled Joseph up out of the cistern and sold him for twenty shekels of silver to the Ishmaelites, who took him to Egypt.*

Father's Thoughts: Be prepared – because you don't know what challenge might come your way or how the outcome may change your life. When I was in high school I played in a rock band. Two of the early members were using drugs and that was hurting me and the other members. After I complained about it, a guy who I thought was a friend, jumped me behind the school and hit me several times calling me a 'narc.' As a result, I was even more determined to stay away from drugs. The rest of the band and I went on to cut an album and keep in touch to this day. God used the situation for good.

Sons' Thoughts: The road to our destined purpose will not always be an easy one. We must be prepared to face challenges along the way. But in the end, these challenges will make our destination all the more appreciated when we persevere and shine for the Lord's kingdom.

Discussion Questions: What tough thing have you faced in life that might have a way of shaping you? How can God use those negative situations for your own good and His purpose?

Notes: _____
_____
_____
_____

Wednesday

Verse: Genesis 39:19-21

> *When his master heard the story his wife told him, saying, "This is how your slave treated me," he burned with anger. Joseph's master took him and put him in prison, the place where the king's prisoners were confined. But while Joseph was there in the prison, the LORD was with him; he showed him kindness and granted him favor in the eyes of the prison warden.*

Father's Thoughts: Be prepared – to take a stand for good when others are leading you to evil. I know many men who have been asked to do something illegal or immoral in their work situations. You young men might have been asked to help someone cheat on a test. When you stand up for what is right, refuse to go along, the consequences may be rough. You could get fired or lose a 'friend.' But like Joseph, the Lord is with us when we do His will.

Sons' Thoughts: Our minds provide us with the ability to decipher between what's right and what's wrong. When we are being tempted to do something we know we shouldn't, that little horn goes blaring in the back of our head, sending out warning signals. My challenge is for you to be on the lookout for these situations and follow the warning signals, knowing that pleasing our Father in Heaven is ultimately more important than pleasing those on earth.

Discussion Questions: How do you think you would react if someone asked you to do something you know is wrong? What might happen if you do not do it? Are you prepared to make that stand?

Notes: _____
_____
_____
_____

Thursday

Verse: Genesis 41:41-43

> *So Pharaoh said to Joseph, "I hereby put you in charge of the whole land of Egypt." Then Pharaoh took his signet ring from his finger and put it on Joseph's finger. He dressed him in robes of fine linen and put a gold chain around his neck. He had him ride in a chariot as his second-in-command, and men shouted before him, "Make way!" Thus he put him in charge of the whole land of Egypt.*

Father's Thoughts: Be prepared – for the fact that all the trials you have faced, all the journeys you have made, moves you might have regretted, are working for God's purpose. I look back at my life: why did my parents move me all over the world – it prepared me to be an international business man with opportunities to witness in all corners of the world. Why did that certain job not work out – it got me out of a rut so that I could do something for God that I otherwise would not have been able to do. God is in the details, He is in the plans.

Sons' Thoughts: Joseph had been thrown in a hole by his brothers, sold as a slave, and put in prison after wrongly being accused of sleeping with his master's wife. But now, after all these things had come to pass, God revealed His ultimate plan by placing Joseph in a position of power over all of Egypt. He was there through the good times and the bad times, and His purpose for Joseph began right when he was born, and everything Joseph went through helped him fulfill this position of power.

Discussion Questions: Look back at your life, the things you have done, the places you have been, the good, the bad. How might God be using these things to shape you for His purposes?

Notes:

Friday

Verse: Genesis 45:3-7

> *Joseph said to his brothers, "I am Joseph! Is my father still living?" But his brothers were not able to answer him, because they were terrified at his presence. Then Joseph said to his brothers, "Come close to me." When they had done so, he said, "I am your brother Joseph, the one you sold into Egypt! And now, do not be distressed and do not be angry with yourselves for selling me here, because it was to save lives that God sent me ahead of you. For two years now there has been famine in the land, and for the next five years there will not be plowing and reaping. But God sent me ahead of you to preserve for you a remnant on earth and to save your lives by a great deliverance.*

Father's Thoughts: Be prepared – to share with others that God has a plan for you and that plan is for their benefit too. Joseph looked back and saw God's hand in everything that had happened to him. There were a lot of really bad things that occurred but the end game was for the best. Our friend Sweet lost her battle with cancer this year. Yet, throughout the pain and agony, she served God well and gave the glory to Jesus where it belonged. Through her, lives have been blessed.

Sons' Thoughts: I can easily understand why Joseph's brothers were terrified when he revealed himself to them. They were expecting revenge from the brother they had sold into slavery those many years ago. But Joseph realized how God's hand was at work throughout his life, and how he was now in the position to save the people of God. Everything he dealt with in life had led him to his ultimate purpose, just as we must persevere through all our hardships to fulfill the plan God has laid for each and every one of us.

Discussion Questions: Who do you know that has gone through tough times but still managed to glorify God in the process? How do you think you can do the same?

Notes: _____
_____
_____
_____

Week 49

God's Will for us NOW

There is an old saying that Satan's greatest weapon against man doing what God intended is NOT convincing us that there is no hope, no love or no purpose; rather it's convincing us there is no hurry. We tend to live our lives in a haze of laziness and complacency. Our focus is on ourselves and what we are doing at the time with no heed to God's direction in our lives. God has a purpose and a plan for every young man that will come to Him and that plan starts…..well, yesterday.

What are you doing this next summer, next Christmas break, in your everyday free time. In tithing, God asks us for our "first fruits" and that means the very best of what we have, including our talents and interests as well as our cash. Brian Sims is the pastor of a deaf congregation. He has challenged his members to look for 2.4 hours a day to give to God in some capacity. That is a hefty challenge and one worth looking toward for everyone. Brian has set out to use his personal talents of sign language to create a video translation of the book of John into American Sign because while those who are deaf can read, they read and absorb language differently than the hearing.

Look at your talents and how you use your time. I am not suggesting that you abandon your sports, activities, or hobbies. Instead, look at how you can transform every part of your day into doing God's will, now.

Right now, today, God wants you to fight the fight against sin in your life
- Be men of self control.

Right now, today, God wants you to listen to him and act.
- Be men that heed God's direction.

Right now, today, God wants you to accept the gift promised to all who accept Jesus as his Savior.
- Be men of the Spirit.

Right now, today, God wants you to do great things for Him.
- Be men of faith and hard work.

Right now, today, God wants you to do great things for others.
- Be men of love.

Challenge:
Men: Help your young man identify two or three things he can do right now to glorify God.
Young Men: Take a "talent inventory". Write down ways you can shape your activities to take advantage of your time and talents for God.

God's Will for us NOW

Monday

Verse: Titus 2:11-12

For the grace of God that brings salvation has appeared to all men. It teaches us to say "No" to ungodliness and worldly passions, and to live self-controlled, upright and godly lives in this present age.

Father's Thoughts: You may be too young to remember the famous "just say no to drugs" campaign. The campaign was meant to show anyone who is faced with the temptation of drugs that a little word "NO" can be a powerful tool. So it is with anything that tempts you. Cheating, lying, fighting, sex outside of marriage, smoking, drugs, JUST SAY NO. Your body is so much more valuable to God than to let these things rule you. Being self-controlled means having the courage to walk away.

Sons' Thoughts: There are many things in this world that can lead to sin. And most of the time it's hard to just say no. But as this passage says, we can gain control over these things by counting on God's word to provide us with advice on how to refrain from sin. The Bible is full of help on about every temptation there is to face.

Discussion Questions: How can you and your Christian friends bond together to support each other in saying NO? Have you ever tried to look in the Bible for advice? How did it turn out? How can sin keep you from being effective for Christ today?

Notes: _____
_____
_____
_____

Tuesday

Verse: 1 Samuel 15:22-23

> *But Samuel replied: "Does the LORD delight in burnt offerings and sacrifices as much as in obeying the voice of the LORD? To obey is better than sacrifice, and to heed is better than the fat of rams. For rebellion is like the sin of divination, and arrogance like the evil of idolatry. Because you have rejected the word of the LORD, he has rejected you as king."*

Father's Thoughts: Saul had lost all his humility towards God. He was big, he was bad, he was tough and he was King. He thought he could disobey God and then "make it up" later with a few additional offerings, because, hey, he was the man! This lack of humility in the form of disobedience was the downfall of a man who could have been a great king.

Sons' Thoughts: Many people in today's church like to think that they can pay God off, by coming to church every once in a while, slipping a check into the offering plate, and then going about their business. This is what Saul was trying to do here. Do people really think that God will look down and see a two hundred dollar check and be impressed? It is his money already, so why would you see that as a way to bypass living a true Christian lifestyle?

Discussion Questions: Where have you let pride and disobedience get in the way of obeying God? How can this render you ineffective in your everyday walk with Him?

Notes: _____
_____
_____

Wednesday

Verse: Luke 11:13

> *If you then, though you are evil, know how to give good gifts to your children, how much more will you Father in heaven give the Holy Spirit to those who ask him!"*

Father's Thoughts: Hopefully you do have a great relationship with your earthly father. We are just men. Even as Christian men we will still fall short of being perfect. God the Father loves you with a love that is perfect, a love that is made just for you. As a gift he gives you the Holy Spirit, his own spirit to dwell within you, and that is a gift that is so much better than I could give you.

Sons' Thoughts: There is evil living inside of us, and we can still do good things for each other, so just imagine what God, who is perfect and holy in every way, can give us if we just ask him.

Discussion Questions: Have you asked God for his gift of the Holy Spirit? How does walking in the Spirit help you live for God every day?

Notes: _____

_____
_____
_____

Thursday

Verse: Haggai 1:13-14

> *Then Haggai, the LORD's messenger, gave this message of the LORD to the people: "I am with you," declares the LORD. So the LORD stirred up the spirit of Zerubbabel son of Shealtiel, governor of Judah, and the spirit of Joshua son of Jehozadak, the high priest, and the spirit of the whole remnant of the people. They came and began to work on the house of the LORD Almighty, their God,*

Father's Thoughts: Zerubbabel (aren't you glad your names are simpler) had been given the task of rebuilding the temple in Jerusalem after it had been destroyed and the people taken to exile. When he started, he came under intense pressure from outsiders and lost his nerve. The project sat for many years unfinished. He was discouraged. Then along came Haggai. He reminded him and all of the people that God was with them. It was the encouragement they needed to finish the task.

Sons' Thoughts: Sometimes all we need is a little encouragement. For someone just to tell us, "Hey, I'm with you, man." So just let someone know that you will always be there for them.

Discussion Questions: Are you willing to let people know that God is with them and can help them complete the purpose in their lives? What can discourage you from doing God's will each day?

Notes: _____
_____
_____
_____

Friday

Verse: John 13:34-35

> *"A new command I give you: Love one another. As I have loved you, so you must love one another. By this all men will know that you are my disciples, if you love one another."*

Father's Thoughts: One of the greatest gifts God has given us through Jesus Christ is the brotherhood of believers. As a body, and especially a group of men, we function together for good. In order to do God's perfect will on earth, Christ made it clear we are to love each other; it is how He, and the world, will identify us as His disciples. We need to start today emulating Christ's love through action.

Sons' Thoughts: One of the most basic things that God tells us to do is simply love each other, to show our love for everyone, even our enemies. This sounds easy, but in our day-to-day lives loving each other is really hard to do. It outwardly reflects what God has done in our lives.

Discussion Questions: What do you think it means to love our brothers in Christ? What are some practical ways we can demonstrate this to those around us?

Notes: _____
_____
_____
_____

Week 50

Getting into the Word – The Importance of the Bible

What a wonderful gift. Right out of college in my first job I got sent to Alaska…..for the winter. No, that wasn't the gift, heck, I froze my tail off. When I arrived in January of 1982, it was 32 below zero. There were about three hours of light per day and, since we worked in windowless offices, we all went out to lunch together just to see the sun. I was only there for four months, but, as a young Christian, I made a point to seek out a church home and found one at First Baptist, Anchorage. The singles group was very active and I soon had a group of friends that I desperately needed and cherished.

When I left that April to go to East Tennessee for my next job assignment I took two new things with me: a Lab/Husky mixed puppy that I had rescued from the cold, and an NIV Study Bible that rescued me from the cold. I loved this particular Bible and the commentaries it contained. This was the point that I turned from just reading the Bible to studying and absorbing it. It was a real turning point in my life and it was not the instrument itself, it was my attitude towards it that changed. It may not take a specific Bible translation to get the juices flowing for you, but whatever it takes to get you excited about God's word, go find it.

The Word of God is meant to challenge you.
- Watch out for the sharp edges.

Not man's word, but God's
- What will it Prophet you.

What do you use to challenge people's thoughts?
- Look to the experts.

It is never too early or never too late to get into the Word.
- It's time to get started.

Being a student of the Bible means, well, going to class.
- Going for proper instruction.

Challenge:
Men: Lead the way in your household by making study of the Bible a top priority both individually and collectively.
Young Men: It is never too early to begin your Christian training. Go read the text, the training manual, the instruction book. Make it a habit.

Getting into the Word – The Importance of the Bible

Monday

Verse: Hebrews 4:12

> *For the word of God is living and active. Sharper than any double-edged sword, it penetrates even to dividing soul and spirit, joints and marrow; it judges the thoughts and attitudes of the heart.*

Father's Thoughts: The Bible is not for wimps. If you are going to be a young man dedicated to the cause of Christ, then you have to be strong and dedicated enough to read the Scriptures and to act upon them. The Bible will reveal things about yourself and others that will be tough to take, but if acted on will change your life and the lives of others.

Sons' Thoughts: God's Word is extremely powerful. It has caused families to be split apart, wars to be started and waged, and lives to be drastically changed spiritually. Words are very influential, and when we are talking about the Word of God itself, we are not dealing with mere literature, but something that will truly define your life.

Discussion Questions: What stories of the Bible make it come alive and seem most real to you? Do you ever feel guilty reading them? What do they reveal about your own personality or actions?

Notes: _____
_____
_____
_____

Tuesday

Verse: 2 Peter 1 19-21

> *And we have the word of the prophets made more certain, and you will do well to pay attention to it, as to a light shining in a dark place, until the day dawns and the morning star rises in your hearts. Above all, you must understand that no prophecy of Scripture came about by the prophet's own interpretation. For prophecy never had its origin in the will of man, but men spoke from God as they were carried along by the Holy Spirit.*

Father's Thoughts: This book you are reading now is man-made, there are many written things in this world that will vie for your attention. It is a bit of a mystery that God inspired the writing of His Word. Face it, these guys were human and were sinners just like you and me. However, they opened themselves up to the inspiration of the Holy Spirit and brought us words of history, hope and challenge. Above all other writings then, the Bible should get your attention.

Sons' Thoughts: We as humans make mistakes, and therefore nothing written by us can be perfect and can certainly not be taken as absolute truth, so God had to come down to them and tell them what to say through the Holy Spirit. We must understand that this is the Holy Word of God and that as such we need to hold it in the highest of regards.

Discussion Questions: Why would God have thought it so important to have a written 'instruction manual'? Why do you think he chose men to write certain things?

Notes: _____
_____
_____
_____

Wednesday

Verse: Acts 17:11-12

Now the Bereans were of more noble character than the Thessalonians, for they received the message with great eagerness and examined the Scriptures every day to see if what Paul said was true. Many of the Jews believed, as did also a number of prominent Greek women and many Greek men.

Father's Thoughts: There will be men in every generation that will say they bring a message from God. The Bereans had the right idea, that is, to challenge whatever someone says with the Scriptures. Is the message preached, is the direction given consistent with what the Bible says about God? By challenging with the Scriptures we can avoid being taken in by charlatans.

Sons' Thoughts: We need to be diligent to listen to those who teach us, but we also need to be able to study the Word and the message ourselves. This not only teaches us to look out for faulty teaching, but to really dig into the Word ourselves. By looking into something that we have already been taught, it teaches us what to look for in the scriptures.

Discussion Questions: When someone tells you they know something, or tries to speak with authority, how do you know that what they are saying is true? You 'look it up,' right? Do you do the same when someone talks about God or spiritual things?

Notes: _____
_____
_____
_____

Thursday

Verse: 2 Timothy 3:14-15

But as for you, continue in what you have learned and have become convinced of, because you know those from whom you learned it, and how from infancy you have known the holy Scriptures, which are able to make you wise for salvation through faith in Christ Jesus.

Father's Thoughts: Some people may have been very young when they first started reading the Bible, having grown up in church and a Christian home. For others it may be later in life. No matter how old you are, from the earliest time you believe, it is good to get into the Word and make it part of your life. Wisdom is a wonderful thing to have – read Proverbs if you have any questions.

Sons' Thoughts: This is how we need to grow in our spiritual walks: We need to remember what we have learned and continue to build upon it, becoming more and more like Christ by reading and obeying His word.

Discussion Questions: When is the youngest time you remember reading the Bible? Do you try to read it often? Do you think it is important to make it a habit?

Notes: _____
_____
_____
_____

Friday

Verse: 2 Timothy 3:16-17

> *All Scripture is God-breathed and is useful for teaching, rebuking, correcting and training in righteousness, so that the man of God may be thoroughly equipped for every good work.*

Father's Thoughts: Teaching: ah, but you have to be willing to be taught and willingness means taking the time to study. Rebuking: it is really hard to face an angry mob if you don't know your authority. Correcting: how can you correct something if you don't know the right way to do it? Training: muscles are not built without exercise and proper nutrition. Now, once trained, go out and do some good, then come back for more.

Sons' Thoughts: We tend to use the Bible for only one or two of the things that Paul suggests that it is good for. We either use it for our own spiritual gain, or as an excuse to rebuke others for misgivings that they might have. What we should use the Bible for is all of the things that it can be used for, and this includes teaching, rebuking, correcting, and training. Only by doing all of this will we be able to live up to our potential for the kingdom of God.

Discussion Questions: What are some tough situations that you face every day that test your faith in God? How could knowing scriptures help you in these times?

Notes: _____
_____
_____
_____

Week 51

Reaching Out — Helping the Poor

When I was ten years old my father's job moved us to Japan. It began a journey that lasted seven years, with subsequent moves to Taiwan and Singapore, but the journey has really lasted a lifetime. Today I continue to be involved in international business and in international missions as the Lord gives me the opportunity. If I learned anything from those years in Asia and from travel is to be aware of the situations and needs of others. I saw deep poverty in parts of Asia, I have seen it here in America as well. I have seen bitter people in Asia, I have seen them in America as well. I have also seen joyous, fun-loving people from all walks of life and from all circumstances. Most of all, I have seen people everywhere that need our Lord and Savior Jesus Christ.

How you approach your fellow man as a Christian ought to be different from those who are non-Christian. We all see others around us who need help, but our desire to help them should come out of our deep love for Christ and in turn, the love He gives us for others. Generosity should then become a part of who we are in Him. It should extend first to those in our immediate charge, our family, then out to others as God reveals to us the needs of those who cross our paths. Start cultivating that generosity as young Christians and let it become a life's passion to help those in need.

Don't hold back your generosity, waiting for another day.
- Get up and help.

Eliminate the poverty that can occur closest to you.
- It starts at home

Not all the poor are out of work.
- Being a good boss

Helping others should be a deliberate action.
- Make it a habit.

Looking at the world through God's eyes.
- Who gets the good seat

Challenge:

Men: Work with your young men to look beyond their own world. Help them understand the plight of those less fortunate and to have a heart that will be generous and understanding.

Young Men: Find ways that you can work outside yourselves. Begin at a young age to help others, to treat others with love and respect and to be generous with what you have. Find a project that can get you out of your world and help someone else in Jesus' name.

Reaching Out — Helping the Poor

Monday

Verse: Proverbs 3:27-28

> *Do not withhold good from those who deserve it,*
>   *when it is in your power to act.*
> *Do not say to your neighbor,*
>   *"Come back later; I'll give it tomorrow" —*
> *when you now have it with you.*

Father's Thoughts: Generosity is a learned skill. Very few of us are naturally generous; we tend to be accumulators and hoarders. I can't remember from back in my elementary school days whether or not I got a good mark for "Shares and Plays Well with Others," but I hope I did. God wants us not only to be generous to those in need but to do it now in His love out of the abundance he has. The poor can't wait.

Sons' Thoughts: We need to be willing to lend out a helping hand when necessary. When we find ourselves in abundance, and able to help others, we should not hesitate or play with others' emotions to make ourselves seem gracious or better than anyone else. God gave us what we did not even deserve, and that was a relationship with Him. We should not withhold anything from our brothers, because all we have is God's in the first place.

Discussion Questions: Who do you see around you who is in need of something tangible, food, clothing, housing, help with homework? How do you react to seeing this need? What can you do?

Notes: _____
_____
_____
_____

Tuesday

Verse: 1 Timothy 5:3-4

> *Give proper recognition to those widows who are really in need. But if a widow has children or grandchildren, these should learn first of all to put their religion into practice by caring for their own family and so repaying their parents and grandparents, for this is pleasing to God.*

Father's Thoughts: An important aspect of helping the poor is not letting people get there in the first place. I have benefitted from great examples in my own family. My parents' generation made sure that my grandparents were well taken care of throughout their lifetimes. But that is not always the case. God has given us families both to help us and for us to help. These lessons learned in taking care of our own house should then spill over to others in need.

Sons' Thoughts: Family is one of the most important institutions that God has devised for us here on earth. By following the rules of God for marriage and family, we are honoring God. As someone who is not married yet, I can honor this by honoring my parents, and becoming the man of God that I can be right now so that I am prepared to be a family man in the future.

Discussion Questions: Whom do you know in your immediate family that has needs? They may not be without clothes and food, but is there something that you can help them with? How are the elderly in your family cared for?

Notes: _____
_____
_____
_____

Wednesday

Verse: Deuteronomy 24:14-15

> *Do not take advantage of a hired man who is poor and needy, whether he is a brother Israelite or an alien living in one of your towns. Pay him his wages each day before sunset, because he is poor and is counting on it. Otherwise he may cry to the LORD against you, and you will be guilty of sin.*

Father's Thoughts: Many of you young men will become leaders, managers, supervisors and business owners. Those who work for you may be in low paid labor. They may not look like you, talk like you, or think like you, but you need to treat them with respect and fairness. Don't just live by the letter of the law but as employers have an attitude towards your workers that is worthy of Christ your brother.

Sons' Thoughts: This is a problem that is spreading rapidly across America. Cheap labor is being capitalized on and people become extremely prejudiced based on what color the person's skin is and how much money they have. We need to treat each other as equals and love everyone as God's sons and daughters.

Discussion Questions: Have you had a first job yet? How were you treated? How do you or would you like to be treated on the job? Given that, what kind of boss or employer would you like to become?

Notes: _____
_____
_____
_____

Thursday

Verse: Leviticus 19:9-10

> *"'When you reap the harvest of your land, do not reap to the very edges of your field or gather the gleanings of your harvest. Do not go over your vineyard a second time or pick up the grapes that have fallen. Leave them for the poor and the alien. I am the LORD your God.*

Father's Thoughts: In everything you do, be deliberately generous. You may not live an agrarian life but you should always find ways to help the poor. Encourage your church to create active programs to help the poor, either directly or through other missions that focus on this area. The key is focusing on the need and with all generosity meeting that need. Whenever possible, become personally involved in the good works for the poor and needy.

Sons' Thoughts: Do not be obsessive over things where you can potentially help others out. For example, if you have food left over that is unopened and you don't think that you will need it, give it to the poor instead of just throwing it out. Seek out ways that our overabundance can help others.

Discussion Questions: Have you learned to tithe? Are you willing to give extra every now and then? What are those things that you have been given that you can share?

Notes: _____
_____
_____
_____

Friday

Verse: James 2:1-7

> *My brothers, as believers in our glorious Lord Jesus Christ, don't show favoritism. Suppose a man comes into your meeting wearing a gold ring and fine clothes, and a poor man in shabby clothes also comes in. If you show special attention to the man wearing fine clothes and say, "Here's a good seat for you," but say to the poor man, "You stand there" or "Sit on the floor by my feet," have you not discriminated among yourselves and become judges with evil thoughts?*
>
> *Listen, my dear brothers: Has not God chosen those who are poor in the eyes of the world to be rich in faith and to inherit the kingdom he promised those who love him? But you have insulted the poor. Is it not the rich who are exploiting you? Are they not the ones who are dragging you into court? Are they not the ones who are slandering the noble name of him to whom you belong?*

Father's Thoughts: James was the younger brother of Jesus. His book in the New Testament takes the most practical and pragmatic look at our faith. Helping the poor starts with attitude. If we have an attitude of superiority, that in itself is a sin towards God and man. There may be a natural tendency for us to react negatively towards someone who is dressed poorly and positively towards someone who looks sharp. God's attitude is different. He looks at everyone through the same eyes.

Sons' Thoughts: Some of the nicest people that I have met have been people who many people in the church would have nothing to do with…. hippies, atheists, and the modern equivalent to the "tax collector." We need to embrace these people as the children of God that they are.

Discussion Questions: What do you REALLY think about when you see that poorly dressed man on the street corner or the family that does not live well? Have you thought about how they got there? What is your inner attitude to those who are in trouble?

Notes:

Week 52

Time to Come Clean - Renewal

Y ou blew it. Maybe it was willful defiance, maybe it started out innocently. You did the wrong thing, a very wrong thing that ended up snowballing and getting worse and worse. The initial act led to denial, you tried to cover up what happened, the cover up led to lies and one follows the other, follows the other. It goes from bad to worse to completely out of control.

Then someone hits you out of the blue. They know the truth, they know the lies, they know everything. It hits you in the face, hard. There is no more running, no more hiding, you are caught. Will you keep trying to cover it up, will you try to discredit the one who knows the truth? You are at a crossroad that every single man has faced and you have to make a choice. You know God is a forgiving God, you know Christ died for you, to forgive your sins. It is time to hit your knees, confess your sin and let God restore you. The consequences of your actions are there, you will have to live with that and work with it, but you can restore yourself to God. As you end the year, take the time to follow King David's lead and ask — no beg— for forgiveness and begin the process of renewal.

- The need to be restored
- A cry for mercy
- The comeback kid

- Inside/Out
- Mr. Clean

Challenge:

Men: You know what trials, falls, and traps are on the road for a young Christian man. Make it clear to your young man that Christ's message of forgiveness is as real as anything that Christ taught.

Young Men: Learn that our God is a loving and forgiving God. You know that you will have problems and you will fall from time to time. Open your heart and mind to God's forgiveness and allow Him to clean you from the inside out.

Time to Come Clean - Renewal

Monday

Verse: Psalm 51:10-12

> *Create in me a pure heart, O God, and renew a steadfast spirit within me. Do not cast me from your presence or take your Holy Spirit from me. Restore to me the joy of your salvation and grant me a willing spirit, to sustain me.*

Father's Thoughts: Once we have been restored to God through his forgiveness it's like we have just hit the break on a runaway car. We have stopped the car and feel safe again, but we have lost momentum. Now we need to renew and restore our relationship with God to get our lives moving. I have seen friends who have been sorry for what they have done and then just sit there and never get back to living. Through Christ we can have that joy back, the joy that really defines a Christian, the joy that sets us apart from a very joy- deprived world.

Sons' Thoughts: We all sin. It is how we deal with the sin that marks our relationship with God. Do we see ourselves as hopeless failure or do we accept God's forgiveness and strive not to repeat it?

Discussion Questions: Have you let some sin, even after you have asked for forgiveness, rob you of the joy of salvation?

Notes: _____
_____
_____
_____

Tuesday

Verse: Psalm 51:1-2

> *Have mercy on me, O God, according to your unfailing love; according to your great compassion blot out my transgressions. Wash away all my iniquity and cleanse me from my sin.*

Father's Thoughts: Have you ever gotten what you deserve? You remember, the time you were punished because…well, because you did it. You messed up, you lied, you stole, you hit, you hurt, you did whatever they said you did and you got caught. Now you have to face the music. Well, David got caught, he committed the crime, he blew it. Now he has to face the music and beg God to forgive him, have mercy on him and not punish him to the full extent he deserves. God wants us to come to Him for forgiveness, He wants to clean us up and hold us in His lap and comfort us. We have all sinned, we all need to say the same prayer as David.

Sons' Thoughts: God is the master of love. Like your parents say when you do something disobedient, "We don't love you any less, but we are disappointed in you." Ouch. I know how that one feels and it's even worse than yelling. God does not love you any less, and once you ask Him for forgiveness, it is like that particular incident never happened.

Discussion Questions: Do you believe that God is a forgiving God and that no matter what you have done, no matter what punishment you really deserve, he will forgive you?

Notes: _____
_____
_____

Wednesday

Verse: Psalm 51:13

Then I will teach transgressors your ways, and sinners will turn back to you.

Father's Thoughts: Being restored back to God, while being a private thing between you and God, can also be a platform for sharing your faith. You are surrounded by other teenagers who struggle with the same issue, who screw up, who sin, just like you. When they see the change in your life that God's mercy brings, the change of salvation in your life, it opens the door for you to share your experience. When you have had mercy given to you, it is time to give it away to that girl in your class, that guy on your team, that neighbor.

Sons' Thoughts: Though we sin and always will, we can be tools for God to use to teach others the errors of their ways and how God's forgiveness blocks out everything, no matter how bad or hurtful.

Discussion Questions: Are you ready to become a teacher of God's ways? Will you share the mercy God has shown you?

Notes: _____
_____
_____
_____

Thursday

Verse: Psalm 51:6

Surely you desire truth in the inner parts you teach me wisdom in the inmost place.

Father's Thoughts: Have you been to a school play lately? It can be a lot of fun to act out, to put on a costume, for a brief moment, take on another personality. Some kids don't need a stage to take on a different character. For some teenagers acting is a way of life and you never really know what is going on inside their head, their heart. God wants to look right through all that. He wants to look right into your heart and get down to the truth. That is where the relationship lies, deep inside you where the entire fake is gone.

Sons' Thoughts: In your innermost thoughts is where God wants to be. When you are making any decision, no matter how small, God wants you to think about "what Jesus would do" no matter how cliché that might sound.

Discussion Questions: Is there a part of your life where you are covering up, holding back, pretending and not being truthful with God?

Notes: _____
_____
_____
_____

Friday

Verse: Psalm 51:7-9

Cleanse me with hyssop, and I will be clean; wash me, and I will be whiter than snow.

Father's Thoughts: Somewhere in your high school career you will read Shakespeare's *Macbeth*. Lady Macbeth took part in a murder and her guilt is so overwhelming that she sleepwalks and tries to wipe imaginary blood off her hands. She couldn't do it. The guilty stains are there in her mind and in her heart. David knew that his only hope to wash away the guilt was the forgiveness of God. He also knew that by fully trusting God's mercy the cleansing would be total; it would be "whiter than snow."

Sons' Thoughts: God forgives us, but we have to be able to accept forgiveness. We have to see ourselves as brand new beings, no longer the way that we were before we were forgiven.

Discussion Questions: It is easy to feel guilty after you have sinned. Do you believe that God can totally forgive you? Can you forgive yourself?

Notes: _____
_____
_____

Printed in the United States
208758BV00003B/70-1176/P